Public Relations *Online*

Public Relations *Online*

Lasting Concepts for Changing Media

Tom Kelleher
University of Hawai'i at Manoa

Copyright © 2007 by Sage Publications, Inc.

All rights reserved. No part of this book may be reproduced or utilized in any form or by any means, electronic or mechanical, including photocopying, recording, or by any information storage and retrieval system, without permission in writing from the publisher.

For information:

Sage Publications, Inc.
2455 Teller Road
Thousand Oaks, California 91320
E-mail: order@sagepub.com

Sage Publications Ltd.
1 Oliver's Yard
55 City Road
London EC1Y 1SP
United Kingdom

Sage Publications India Pvt. Ltd.
B-42, Panchsheel Enclave
Post Box 4109
New Delhi 110 017 India

Printed in the United States of America

Library of Congress Cataloging-in-Publication Data

Kelleher, Tom (Tom A.)
  Public relations online : lasting concepts for changing media / Tom Kelleher.
      p. cm.
  Includes bibliographical references and index.
  ISBN 1-4129-1417-5 or 978-1-4129-1417-8 (pbk.)
  1. Public relations—Data processing. 2. Public relations—Computer network resources. I. Title.

HM1221.K45 2007
659.20285′4678—dc22   2006025770

This book is printed on acid-free paper.

07 08 09 10 10 9 8 7 6 5 4 3 2 1

Acquisitions Editor:	Todd R. Armstrong
Editorial Assistant:	Sarah K. Quesenberry
Production Editor:	Libby Larson
Copy Editor:	Julie Gwin
Typesetter:	C&M Digitals (P) Ltd.
Proofreader:	Ellen Brink
Indexer:	Michael Ferreira
Cover Designer:	Glenn Vogel

Brief Contents

Preface   **xiii**

Chapter 1: Interactive Public Relations   1

Chapter 2: Systems Everywhere   15

Chapter 3: Server-Side Public Relations   29

Chapter 4: Peer-to-Peer Public Relations   43

Chapter 5: Relationships   59

Chapter 6: News-Driven Relationships   75

Chapter 7: Commerce-Driven Relationships   89

Chapter 8: Issue-Driven Relationships   105

Chapter 9: Managing Public Relations in Real Time   123

Chapter 10: Applied Research and Evaluation   137

Index   **153**

About the Author   **161**

Contents

Preface   **xiii**

Note to Students xiii

Note to Teachers and Professionals xiii

Text Overview—Seeking Lasting Concepts xiv

Acknowledgments xv

Chapter 1. Interactive Public Relations   **1**

Overview 1

Where to Start? 1

De-hyping Hypermedia 2

Defining Online Media 4

Public Relations and the "De-massification" of Media 8

Interactivity and Real People 10

References 12

Hands-Online Activity: Did You Hear? 14

Chapter 2. Systems Everywhere   **15**

Overview 15

Systems Online 15

What Makes a System? 16

Putting the Systems Vocabulary to Work 18

Systems, Online Media, and the Day-to-Day
    Roles of Public Relations People 20

Questionable Claims: It's All "Pull" Media Now! 23

Why Systems Theory Matters for Online Public
Relations (and Why We Need Other Theories, Too) 24

References 25

Hands-Online Activity: Linking Systems 27

Chapter 3. Server-Side Public Relations   29

Overview 29

Server-Side Public Relations 30

One-Way Approaches to Online Public Relations 30

Practitioner Typologies 32

Gathering, Packaging, Disseminating 34

*Questionable Claims: The Internet Grew Faster
Than Any Medium in History!* 35

One-Way Tactics and Interactive Public Relations 39

References 40

*Hands-Online Activity: What's New in Online
Public Relations?* 41

Chapter 4. Peer-to-Peer Public Relations   43

Overview 43

Peer-to-Peer Public Relations 44

Two-Way Models 45

Two-Way Typologies 47
Dialogue 49
Markets as Conversations—Another
Perspective on "PR Types" 52
It Depends 53

References 54

Hands-Online Activity: Cases in Point? 56

Chapter 5. Relationships   59

Overview 59

Focusing on Relationships 59

Not-So-Secret Ingredients for Success—
Relational Antecedents 60

Building and Maintaining Relationships—
Relational Processes 66

Evaluating Relational Strategies—
Relationship Outcomes 67

References 70

Hands-Online Activity: Lurk and Learn 73

Chapter 6. News-Driven Relationships 75

Overview 75

Publicity in the Big Picture 75

Online Media Relations—What Needs
to Be in Place? 76
Technology and Content 76

*Questionable Claims: Using Online Media to
Cut Out the Middleman* 78
Journalists as People—Pushing, Pulling,
Tugging, Dancing 82
Culture in Media Relations 83

Making Yourself Useful 85

References 86

Hands-Online Activity: Newsworthiness Online 88

Chapter 7. Commerce-Driven Relationships 89

Overview 89

What Needs to Be in Place? 90
Technology and Content 90
People and the Cultures of
Online Commerce 95

Questionable Claims: None of Our Business? 100

References 100

*Hands-Online Activity: Do-It-Yourself
FAQ Tips* 102

Chapter 8. Issue-Driven Relationships   **105**

Overview 105

Issues and Online Organizations and Publics 106

What Needs to Be in Place? 106
    Technology and Content 107
    Individuals—Putting the Active in
      Interactive Media 108
    Active Social Networks 109

Shifting From Active Publics to Active Organizations 112

Relational Goals and Outcomes 113

Making Peace 117

References 118

Hands-Online Activity: Truth or Consequences 120

Chapter 9. Managing Public Relations in Real Time   **123**

Overview 123

The Speed of Real Time 124

Planning 124

*Questionable Claims: Instant Synergy—Just Add
  Technology?* 129

Action and Communication Processes 130

References 133

Hands-Online Activity: Blogs and Strategy 135

Chapter 10. Applied Research and Evaluation   **137**

Overview 137

The Value in Evaluation 138

Surveys 139

Experiments 141

Interviews and Focus Groups 142

Usability 145

Unobtrusive Methods 145

What to Evaluate 148

References 148

Hands-Online Activity: Online Research 150

Index   **153**

About the Author   **161**

Preface

❖ NOTE TO STUDENTS

Sitting down to write this book, I was reminded of countless textbooks I've read that start with some variation on the following, "[Insert field name here] is everywhere you look." In elementary school, math was everywhere I looked. In middle school, geography surrounded me. Physics moved me and biology made me in high school. Language defined me in my early years of college. And when I chose communication as a major, I learned that communication was, well, everywhere I looked.

Yes, online communication seems to be almost everywhere you look in public relations. And like the better texts in math, geography, physics, and language that use theory to help us make better sense of things we see every day, I hope this book helps you make sense of the public relations in front of you every time you go online.

❖ NOTE TO TEACHERS AND PROFESSIONALS

I've written this book to help us look at online public relations like public relations scholars do, which means taking an excited interest in the Internet, but also taking care not to overstate its implications. Theory and context are crucial to helping us make sense of why and how public relations people choose and use rapidly emerging technological innovation.

"Questionable Claims" boxes throughout the text take alternative perspectives on sometimes-taken-for-granted cyber-declarations. I'm certain that time (and reviewers) will find me guilty of some "questionable claims" myself. In any case, I hope these cases serve to help us all sharpen our critical-thinking skills. (I just did a Google search for

xiii

critical thinking and *syllabus* and *public relations*—it yielded 8,690 results in 0.11 seconds.) Furthermore, the questionable claims are not all straw men—some hold up better than others after critical review.

❖ TEXT OVERVIEW—SEEKING LASTING CONCEPTS

Blogs were barely on my academic radar when I started writing this book, and I certainly had never seen a corporate blog posted by a CEO. My iPod mini wasn't set up for automatic downloads of weekly podcasts of my favorite news shows. In fact, Apple hadn't even introduced the iPod mini to the market. U.S. corporations filing financial reports were not yet required to comply with the more stringent disclosure requirements of the Sarbanes-Oxley Act, which was passed to improve accuracy, reliability, and ultimately trust in corporate America. So XBRL (extensible business reporting language) as an online technology for keeping in compliance with the act had not been tested. (The implications of XBRL, discussed in Chapter 7, are still yet to be determined.) In a very observable way, technology and policy have moved faster than the speed of book writing.

Yet relative to iPods and XBRL, systems theory, two-way communication, and relational approaches to public relations are sources of lasting concepts. These theoretical ideas are not immutable, but they do give us relatively stable lenses through which to explore online public relations. Perhaps the greatest test of the validity of these concepts is how well they stay grounded as the media landscape changes. I've tried to write this book as a model for how such lasting concepts can be discussed and applied in a changing media environment.

In general, this text moves from more theoretical discussion in earlier chapters to more practical lessons in later chapters, with the idea that useful theory informs effective practice even as the media landscape changes. Chapter 1 establishes the optimistic but cautious tone of the book by juxtaposing historical accounts of mass media effects to often-overstated claims about the Internet. Examples of online media are offered and a theme is developed for the text—online public relations is more a matter of what people are doing with online media technologies than what these technologies are doing to people.

Chapter 2 reviews systems theory as it can be used to describe online public relations processes. Chapter 3 discusses online public relations in terms of "server-side" practices in which organizations deliver information to their publics. Chapter 4 contrasts the server-side metaphor with a peer-to-peer model in which organizations and publics are involved in a more balanced online exchange of information and resources.

Chapter 5 offers an overview of relational approaches—the "relations" part of public relations online. The next three chapters (6, 7, and 8) shift to more specific practical issues of online relationships: news-driven relationships, commerce-driven relationships, and issue-driven relationships.

Chapter 9 builds on familiar concepts of strategic planning, discussing how goals and objectives can be met through online action and communication. Online research and evaluation tie together the ends of the loop-like process of online public relations. Chapter 10 concludes the text by discussing some of the ways public relations people can do research online to assess the outcomes of their work.

❖ ACKNOWLEDGMENTS

I'd like to thank all my friends and colleagues in the School of Communications at the University of Hawai'i and in the School of Journalism & Mass Communication at the University of North Carolina at Chapel Hill for their support while I wrote; the editors and staff at Sage for guiding me through from proposal to print; my teachers at the University of Florida for guiding my intellectual interests; and above all, my parents and family for their endless support.

In addition, Sage Publications and I wish to thank the following reviewers:

W. Timothy Coombs, Eastern Illinois University; Kirk Hallahan, Colorado State University; Robert L. Heath, University of Houston; Edward J. Lordan, West Chester University of Pennsylvania; Bonita Dostal Neff, Valparaiso University; and Jim Pokrywczynski, Marquette University.

For Robin and Miles

1

Interactive Public Relations

❖ OVERVIEW

Technologies for online public relations are introduced. The function of public relations is connected with the concept of interactivity. Building on prior mass communication scholarship, a theme is developed for the text that approaching online public relations is more a matter of what people are doing with online media technologies than what these technologies are doing to people.

❖ WHERE TO START?

Perhaps a colorful vignette is a good place to start a book on online public relations.

She wakes up by the alarm on her PDA and checks e-mail and a couple of podcasts while slurping down a cup of coffee. Then she races off to her office, which is actually the spare bedroom in her apartment. After adjusting the Web cam and microphone on her desktop, she chimes into her first meeting of the day with fellow account executives in Europe and South America as well as some of her colleagues in the United States. An instant message from a reporter pops up on her monitor while she watches a real-time PowerPoint presentation on the best way to launch her client's new social networking site.

With the rate of change in media technology, we might as well start with:

He gets to the office at 9 A.M. His secretary hands him a facsimile from the New York office that rolled off the spool the night before. It's a news release on the launch of an affordable cellular telephone that fits easily in an average brief-case. While he waits for his high-performance 486 to boot up, he reads through a couple of newspapers and slurps down his coffee. (We can't have our busy powerbrokers just "sip" coffee.) *His modem buzzes and beeps and screeches as it connects to the Internet at a blazing 14,400 bits per second. . . .*

Although the first vignette shows some progress made since the second example, both are snapshots that will seem equally dated in a few short years (if they don't already).

Another approach might be to herald the dramatic changes the Internet has made to public relations and to society as a whole. This way, we can avoid getting caught up with the messy specifics of technology that change faster than the publishing cycle of books like this one.

The Internet revolution is here! Strap yourself in and hang on for a wild ride as our field and our world change at an accelerated pace never before experienced by mankind. Public relations will never be the same, and neither will you . . . Online media are everywhere you look.

The hype itself sounds dated. And, of course, in a field often criticized for hyperbole, we have to be especially careful not to overstate the implications of the new technologies we embrace.

❖ DE-HYPING HYPERMEDIA

Getting beneath the hype has been an issue for those studying communication since the early days of mass communication scholarship.

In October 1938, Orson Welles's and Howard Koch's radio adaptation of H. G. Wells's *War of the Worlds* panicked some Americans.

People in New Jersey fled into the streets with wet rags on their faces to protect themselves from the Martians' noxious heat rays, doctors and nurses offered police their assistance to aid the victims, and hospitals treated real patients for shock and hysteria (Sourcebooks, 2001). Moreover, *War of the Worlds* helped hype the "mass-ness" of mass media. For most people who experienced or read about the Welles broadcast shortly thereafter, the *War of the Worlds* fiasco just underscored the powerful effects of media (Lowery & DeFleur, 1995).

But Hadley Cantril (1940) formed a different opinion, one that helped lay groundwork for generations of mass communication scholars. Cantril's research on the way audiences responded to the radio broadcast is considered a milestone in mass communication research today because it clearly undermined the so-called "magic bullet" theory of mass media. He found that different people responded differently to the broadcast, largely based on factors such as critical thinking (e.g., many listeners simply checked other news sources). As we will see, the research that informs much of our look at online public relations builds on the ideas that different people make different uses of media and that the study of mass media and public relations now usually overlaps with the study of interpersonal communication (Coombs, 2001).

Newer media sometimes panic publics too. In 1999, we were really concerned about the Y2K problem. In the United States, the CIA advised its employees to stockpile cash and pay bills early. As fears about the collapse of the nation's digital infrastructure mounted, businesses providing bulk foods, generators, and any other items a survivalist might find handy saw enormous increases in sales (McCullagh, 1999a, 1999b). Whereas media content was the primary culprit in the *War of the Worlds* episode, media technology is what people feared with the Y2K issue. What if the network of computers that comprise the Internet were to crash?

Fortunately, the Y2K missile was a dud. Writing for the University of Southern California, Annenberg's, *Online Journalism Review,* Scheer (2000) said:

> The Y2K crisis should serve as a cautionary tale in evaluating all aspects of the much-ballyhooed Internet age that is upon us. The changes implied by a wired world are indeed profound, but they are not, as the Y2K alarmists insisted, of inevitable Earth-shattering proportions. We've lived with computers long enough to know that as with other technological revolutions, life goes on pretty much as it did before.

4   Public Relations Online

Far from panic, the Internet also has been the subject of grand expectations by pundits from many corners of the global political map in the early 2000s. Progressives have hoped the Internet would act as a political participation machine, mobilizing the voiceless masses to get involved in political discourse. Conservatives have seen the Internet as a free-market competitor to traditional mass media, relaxing the need for tight government regulation on media ownership and content, but as Internet-and-society researchers Cooper and Cooper put it in 2003, "After two decades of presence in civil society, the Internet has not lived up to its hope or hype" (p. i).

Yet somewhere between hype and apathy, lasting lessons are waiting to be learned. Early mass communication researchers used the tools of psychology and public opinion research to understand the lasting implications of the changing media landscape of their time. This book discusses how public relations academics and professionals, borrowing from a wide variety of related disciplines, are working to discover the lasting implications of online media for their field.

❖ DEFINING ONLINE MEDIA

Web sites, e-mail, intranets, Internet forums, wikis, and blogs look and act a lot different than the media of early mass communication research such as newspapers, books, radio, and television. E-mail and blogs, for example, are usually more about interpersonal communication than mass communication. But as communication science pioneer Wilbur Schramm (1973) noted decades ago, and decades before the Internet, the distinction between mass communication and interpersonal communication is largely arbitrary:

> Indeed, it could be argued that many qualities of an inflammatory face-to-face speech to a mob are less personal, more mass, than a singer crooning through a radio into the ear of a teen-ager alone in her room. (p. 114)

In this text, the term *online media* will be used to cover a broad range of communication systems, channels, and formats. Some, such as instant messaging, may be used for very interpersonal purposes, whereas others, such as high-traffic Web pages, are designed to reach masses. In a sense, the Internet is *the* medium for online communication, and technologies like instant messaging and the Web represent the systems, channels, formats, and messages that it contains. In this text, the term *online media* will comprise all of these elements of Internet communication technology. Here is a set of definitions to get us started.

Internet. The Internet is a global network of publicly accessible networks. It's the worldwide system of computers, cables, and wired and wireless devices that connect to each other to help people and machines exchange information. For the purposes of this book, if communication is happening on the Internet, then it's happening online.

World Wide Web. The Web is a collection of resources available for us to retrieve with our Web browsers. These resources (e.g., Web pages) often are formatted with hypertext, which allows users to click on a word or image to retrieve another resource. Uniform resource locators (URLs) are the working Internet addresses for such Web resources. Of course, these resources can be audio files or 3-D animations or video, as well as text and pictures. We all know the Web when we see it, but it is important to realize that the Web is only part of the Internet.

FTP, or file transfer protocol. FTP allows users to put files on a computer server that other people can then retrieve from different locations. As with Web browsing and Web downloading, this transfer of files happens on the Internet. An FTP program can be used instead of a Web browser. Such file transfer sites have URLs that start with "ftp" instead of "http," which stands for "hypertext transfer protocol." Organizations can host an FTP site to make just about any type of computer file available for download. Millions of pages of documents, software programs, multimedia files, and databases that might have required a warehouse and several clerks to physically dig through stacks of information every time someone requested a document, film, or spreadsheet now can be stored and retrieved on a server machine stashed in a hall closet. Files to be transferred can be password protected or made accessible to any anonymous computer user who knows the FTP address.

E-mail. E-mail programs allow users to compose, send, and retrieve messages formatted for electronic delivery as well as attachments formatted for an array of uses such as text documents, photos, spreadsheets, and audio and video files. E-mail is generally thought of as an asynchronous mode of communication. That is, generally the senders and receivers need not be online at the same time for e-mail to work. If you send someone an e-mail, you normally don't assume that they will see the message and respond instantly when you hit "send." For text-based conversations that need to happen in real time (more like phone calls), online chats might be a better option.

Chats and instant messaging. Internet relay chats and instant messaging systems work like e-mail programs in that they can be used for one-to-one communication or for one-to-many communication. They

6   Public Relations Online

also can be used for many-to-many communication, depending on the number of people included as senders and receivers. The main difference is that the term *chat* in online contexts usually means instant, text-based communication. Since online chats and instant messages still are not quite as "instant" as phone calls or face-to-face conversations—they require at least the amount of time it takes to type a message and send it—many-to-many online chats can be frustrating when several users try to "talk" at once.

Internet forums. These are sometimes called discussion forums, bulletin board systems, newsgroups, or message boards. These systems provide virtual places where people can post comments or questions, which in turn start conversational threads. A thread may start with a single question that goes unanswered for a while until someone posts a single response, or it may almost immediately ignite a heated debate in which many interested users get involved. Forums are generally set up to host conversations dedicated to particular topics. Like e-mail, and unlike chats, forums are generally designed for asynchronous communication.

Intranets and extranets. Intranets are networked information systems that an organization hosts for its internal publics. A business might host an intranet for people who work there. This site might include a directory of employee contact information, sales databases, internal classified ads, announcements about workplace events, an internal messaging program, discussion groups for departmental issues, downloadable human resource documents such as health insurance forms, photo galleries of recent social events, how-to video clips, frequently asked questions, and so forth. What sets an intranet apart from a general-access Web page is simply that users must be registered and have a password to participate. Sometimes users can be logged on automatically if they're working from a machine that is directly connected to the network. The idea of controlled-access communication is also the foundation for extranets. When two or more organizations link intranets, or when an organization extends intranet access to a group such as suppliers, vendors, customers, or other businesses to share data and open communication between members, an extranet is formed.

Content management systems and Wikis.

A content management system (CMS) is a computer software system for organizing and facilitating collaborative creation of documents and other content. A content management system is frequently a web application used for managing websites and web content. (Wikipedia contributors, 2005)

This definition comes from Wikipedia, which is itself a content management system. Wikipedia allows people from all over the world to register and edit its content. In 2005, The Wikipedia Foundation boasted that more than a half million "wikipedians" had contributed to the endeavor. Although Wikipedia represents one of the most massive attempts at a CMS, many public relations people are looking to more focused CMSs, commonly called "wikis," to meet their goals of managing information online (as discussed in Chapter 9).

Here's Wikipedia's definition of a wiki:

A type of website that allows users to easily add, remove, or otherwise edit all content, very quickly and easily, sometimes without the need for registration. This ease of interaction and operation makes a wiki an effective tool for collaborative writing. The term wiki is a shortened form of *wiki wiki* which is from the native language of Hawaii (Hawaiian), where it is commonly used as an adjective to denote something "quick" or "fast." (Wikipedia contributors, 2006)

Blogs. Merriam-Webster Online (n.d.) named *blog* (short for "Web log") their word of the year in 2004, and defined it in their *Collegiate Dictionary Online* as "a website that contains an online personal journal with reflections, comments, and often hyperlinks provided by the writer." Blogs also have been defined as "frequently modified web pages in which dated entries are listed in reverse chronological sequence" (Herring, Scheidt, Bonus, & Wright, 2004, p. 1).

In late 2004, David Sifry of Technorati, a San Francisco company that tracks blogs, classified approximately 5,000 blogs as "corporate blogs." *Corporate bloggers*, as defined by Sifry, are "people who blog in an official or semi-official capacity at a company, or are so affiliated with the company where they work that even though they are not officially spokespeople for the company, they are clearly affiliated." Bloggers who worked for Microsoft made up the largest single group of corporate bloggers at the time. The other major groups of corporate bloggers were from media companies such as newspapers and magazines, as well as other major players in the computer industry such as Sun Microsystems.

Although this snapshot data doesn't adequately portray the dynamic nature of evolving blog demographic trends, it does go to show how blogging emerged from the world of computer programmers and hobbyists and into the lexicon of everyday public relations.

Feeds and really simple syndication (RSS). Feeds carry messages such as text-based blog entries or audio files that are syndicated to subscribers online after they are posted. A key difference between

8   Public Relations Online

syndication in this context on the Internet and subscriptions in traditional mass media contexts is that almost all this information is transferred without fees (at least for now). Subscribers use programs called
aggregators to automatically retrieve and display feeds. Aggregators
can display feeds on personalized Web pages, on a user's desktop, or
on a user's wireless handheld device. The computer protocol behind
such aggregators is RSS, which is based on extensible markup language. Feeds downloaded to iPods and other portable digital media
players (as well as laptops and desktops) are called *podcasts.*

Tracking and pings. This is a type of automatic linking used with
online media formats such as blogs. When a blogger links to another
blogger in her post, and both blogs are supported by Trackback technology or the like, the blog that is linked to can be "pinged." A ping is
a notification to one blog that it has that been cited on another blog.
Trackback software can automatically create a list of summaries of blog
posts that refer to an original blog post. Each time the original blog post
is pinged, Trackback adds a summary of the referrer post to the original post. This allows bloggers to track related blogs automatically and
allows blog visitors to jump into a network of blogs that are related to
each other. Tracking and pings have useful applications in the evaluation of public relations efforts.

❖ PUBLIC RELATIONS AND
    THE "DE-MASSIFICATION" OF MEDIA

Funded by the U.S. government during the Cold War, the inventors of
the Internet's first networks figured that one way to protect information critical to the United States' defense system was to spread that
information around. If one location was destroyed in an attack or melt-
down, other locations could continue to communicate. We learned in
the 20th century that diversity is a great defense for the "masses"
against magic bullets. Now in the 21st century, we are seeing the media
themselves distributed in such a way that it is harder to find singular
dominant sources of mass communication. For every conservative
blogger online, there's a liberal. For every Florida Gator, there's a
Georgia Bulldog. For every journalist, a corporate spokesperson.

So here we are, two or three generations of media scholarship since
War of the Worlds, still trying to get beneath the hype. We know that
on the receiver end of the communication process, individuals vary
greatly in how media affect them. But now we are beginning to question

whether the "sender" end of the model is becoming so diverse that the term *mediated communication* may better cover the domains of fields such as public relations, advertising, and journalism.

The late Steven Chaffee, a communication scholar who contributed as much to our knowledge of mass communication as anyone, took the question head on in one of his last lectures and essays:

> In the near future, the issue may be less about what media companies are doing *to* people and more about what people are doing *with* the media . . . as the mass-ness of the media declines and as new technologies continue to empower individuals, social control by elite groups in society may become more difficult. (Chaffee & Metzger, 2001, p. 370)

In terms of social equity, I take Chaffee's measured foresight to be good news, but for the sake of the degrees on my wall, I am glad he didn't pronounce mass communication completely dead. In any case, we need to be more wary than ever of one-size-fits-all thinking. Online public relations is about much more than people in large, powerful organizations using the most expensive new technologies to communicate at relatively powerless publics. In this book, we will explore the underlying concepts that help us understand what public relations practitioners of all sorts are doing with all sorts of online media.

Will the fundamental nature of public relations change as a result of online technologies?

Public relations, defined so well by Cutlip, Center, and Broom (2000) in their classic public relations text, *Effective Public Relations,* as "the management function that identifies, establishes, and maintains mutually beneficial relationships between an organization and the various publics on whom its success or failure depends" has been around a lot longer than the Internet (p. 6). Relationship building is still about people, and the technologies are merely tools that people can use—ideally—to get along better. Nonetheless, these technologies do different things than the media that came before them.

One of the most often-discussed but least-understood characteristics of online media is *interactivity.* Although all good public relations is interactive at some level, online media offer practitioners the opportunity to enrich the interactive exchanges between organizations and publics in the absence of face-to-face communication. Yet with such technological offerings come conceptual challenges, especially if we are after lasting concepts.

Converging mobile technologies that combine the functions of messaging with calendaring, computing, phoning, browsing, purchasing, photography, and entertainment offer a more fluid environment for the practice of public relations. Keeping in touch with the online but wireless publics of "cyber public relations" as part of a relationship-building process means thinking of public relations as a communicative activity that entails "stimulating feelings such as connectedness, involvement, appreciation, and meaningfulness" (Galloway, 2005, p. 573). Such goals pose new challenges in communicating with more physically dispersed publics.

Our home-office worker practicing public relations in the vignette at the outset of this chapter must take into account not only her own unique technologies of connection but also the mobility of those with whom she communicates and the fleeting nature of her publics. Tools for "mobile-based interactivity" must increasingly be considered along with "static reception equipment" (Galloway, 2005, p. 572). And just as Galloway (2005) has called for more "dynamic touch" when communicating via mobile devices, researchers have found that with Web sites, there's an "emotional advantage" to making online communication more interactive—reminiscent of "pressing-the-flesh" (Sundar, Kalyanaraman, & Brown, 2003, p. 31). The best of the new, then, is still driven by concepts as old as conversations and handshakes.

❖ INTERACTIVITY AND REAL PEOPLE

Communication researchers Walther, Gay, and Hancock (2005) put it well when they said that interactivity "is not new to new technology" (p. 640). But just what is interactivity? Sundar et al. (2003) reviewed the research and found two general ways to look at it: *functional interactivity* and *contingency interactivity.*

Functional interactivity. This concept focuses on the features of media such as response forms, e-mail links, discussion forums, RSS, and so forth. Some have assumed that more features mean more interactivity. However, "the degree to which these functions are used and the extent to which they actually serve the dialogue or discourse" is often left out when people think about online media without also thinking about how people actually use the media (Sundar et al., 2003, p. 33).

Contingency interactivity. Media effects researchers describe contingency interactivity as "a process involving users, media and messages" in which "communication roles need to be interchangeable for full interactivity to occur" (Sundar et al., 2003, p. 35). Contingency in this line of research and theory means that messages in an interactive process of communication are contingent on previous messages. The sender now is a receiver later, and vice versa. Broad views of public relations reflect similar thinking.

Contingency public relations. In organization-public relationships, the organization in one case is a public in the next. Of course, if you work in public relations for an organization, as opposed to studying one from outside, you will almost always think of your employer as the "organization" and those you communicate with as publics. But interactive public relations will still mean basing your actions and communication on the actions and communication of those with whom you communicate. If your publics are out there on their BlackBerries and iPods, you'll have to meet them there.

Consider how trends in employee relations, for instance, have been articulated in light of emerging media: "New media have empowered employees to the point where they now can—and do—play a much more dominant role in the communication process . . . receivers are playing a more dominant role in the communication process" (Wright, 2005, p. 9). And how organizations build and maintain relationships with activists might well be the area in which the idea of balanced conversations has come the furthest. Consider the contingency theory of public relations. Public relations strategies and tactics range from aggressive advocacy to total accommodation in contingency theory:

> Experienced professionals know that "it depends." We must always ask what is going to be the most effective method at a given time. True excellence in public relations may result from picking the appropriate point along the continuum that best fits the current need of the organization and its publics. (Cancel, Cameron, Sallot, & Mitrook, 1997, p. 35)

It's no accident of semantics that the contingency view of interactivity and the contingency view of public relations dovetail so well. Good public relations, like good online communication, depends on the situation and the people involved. Emerging communication technologies may "de-massify" public communication, but public relations people should work to ensure technologies don't dehumanize communication. As Chaffee said, the issue is what people are doing with media, not the other way around.

12   Public Relations Online

❖ REFERENCES

Cancel, A. E., Cameron, G. T., Sallot, L. M., & Mitrook, M. A. (1997). It depends: A contingency theory of accommodation in public relations. *Journal of Public Relations Research, 9,* 31–63.

Cantril, H. (1940). *The invasion from Mars: A study in the psychology of panic.* Princeton, NJ: Princeton University Press.

Chaffee, S. H., & Metzger, M. J. (2001). The end of mass communication? *Mass Communication & Society, 4,* 365–379.

Coombs, W. T. (2001). Interpersonal communication and public relations. In R. L. Heath & G. Vasquez (Eds.), *Handbook of Public Relations* (pp. 105–114). Thousand Oaks, CA: Sage.

Cooper, M., & Cooper, S. (2003). Hope and hype v. reality: The role of the commercial Internet in democratic discourse and prospects for institutional change. *Proceedings of the 2003 Telecommunications Policy Research Conference.* Retrieved June 7, 2006, from http://web.si.umich.edu/tprc/papers/2003/213/HOPE&HYPE.pdf

Cutlip, S. M., Center, A. H., & Broom, G. H. (2000). *Effective public relations* (8th ed.) Upper Saddle River, NJ: Prentice Hall.

Galloway, C. (2005). Cyber-PR and "dynamic touch." *Public Relations Review, 31,* 572–577.

Herring, S. C., Scheidt, L. A., Bonus, S., & Wright, E. (2004). Bridging the gap: A genre analysis of weblogs. *Proceedings of the 37th Hawai'i International Conference on System Sciences (HICSS-37).* Los Alamitos, CA: IEEE Computer Society Press.

Lowery, S. A., & DeFleur, M. L. (1995). *Milestones in mass communication research: Media effects* (3rd ed.) White Plains, NY: Longman.

McCullagh, D. (1999a, January 26). Feds plan Y2K spin control. *Wired.* Retrieved June 7, 2006, from http://www.wired.com/news/politics/ 0,1283,17527,00 .html

McCullagh, D. (1999b, February 18). White House fears Y2K panic. *Wired.* Retrieved June 7, 2006, from http://www.wired.com/news/politics/ 0,1283,17986,00.html

Merriam-Webster Online. (n.d.). *Blog.* Available from www.m-w.com

Scheer, R. (2000). The age of the Internet—Hysteria, hyperbole and profit. *Online Journalism Review.* Retrieved June 7, 2006, from http://www.ojr .org/ojr/technology/1017966310.php

Schramm, W. (1973). *Men, messages and media: A look at human communication.* New York: Harper & Row.

Sifry, D. (2004). *Sifry's alerts: Oct 2004 state of the blogosphere.* Retrieved June 7, 2006, from http://www.sifry.com/alerts/archives/000390.html

Sourcebooks. (2001). *The War of the Worlds: Mars' invasion of Earth, inciting panic and inspiring terror from H.G. Wells to Orson Welles and beyond.* Naperville, IL: Author.

Sundar, S. S., Kalyanaraman, S., & Brown, J. (2003). Explicating Web site inter-activity: Impression formation effects in political campaign sites. *Communication Research, 30,* 30–59.

Walther, J. B., Gay, G., & Hancock, J. T. (2005). How do communication and technology researchers study the Internet? *Journal of Communication, 55,* 632–657.

Wikipedia contributors. (2005). Content management system. In *Wikipedia, The Free Encyclopedia.* Retrieved June 7, 2006, from http://en.wikipedia.org/wiki/Content_management_system

Wikipedia contributors. (2006). Wiki. In *Wikipedia, The Free Encyclopedia.* Retrieved June 7, 2006, from http://en.wikipedia.org/w/index.php?title=Wiki&oldid=50085325

Wright, D. K. (2005, March 10–13). *An analysis of the increasing importance of the role of the receiver in the communication process.* Paper presented at the 8th International Public Relations Conference, Miami, FL. Retrieved June 7, 2006, from http://www.instituteforpr.com/pdf/D_Wright_Miami_2005.pdf

14   Public Relations Online

Hands-Online Activity

❖ DID YOU HEAR?

Would Orson Welles be able to pull off *War of the Worlds* with the same effect in today's media environment? Maybe not, but some things haven't changed. As media consumers, we still have our critical-thinking skills tested regularly online.

Subject: FW: Must Read!!!! Bill Gates (fwd)

Hello everybody, My name is Bill Gates. I have just written up an e-mail tracing program that traces everyone to whom this message is forwarded to. I am experimenting with this and I need your help. Forward this to everyone you know and if it reaches 1000 people everyone on the list will receive $1000 at my expense. Enjoy.

Your friend,

Bill Gates

This message was one of the most infamous e-mail hoaxes of the late 1990s. David Emery, who writes about hoaxes and urban legends for About.com, discussed the "robust circulation" of this e-mail at http://urbanlegends.about.com/library/blgates.htm.

Have you ever fallen for an online hoax?

The following Web sites track and discuss Internet hoaxes. Look through these sites or similar online resources. Then answer the discussion questions.

- http://www.breakthechain.org/
- http://www.snopes.com/
- http://urbanlegends.about.com/
- http://www.vmyths.com/

1. Summarize one of the hoaxes that you might classify as a public relations issue. Based on the definition of public relations offered by Cutlip et al. (2000), what makes the hoax a public relations issue?

2. What would you do about that hoax if you worked for the organization involved? Does your response include online media? Why or why not?

2

Systems Everywhere

❖ OVERVIEW

Online networks are described as models illustrating the systems in which public relations people and their publics work and live. Then some basic concepts from systems theory are covered as they apply to online public relations. But understanding computer systems in public relations is only useful to the extent that we consider the social systems these technologies serve. The chapter shifts from looking at computer systems as models for public relations systems to looking at computer systems as tools for public relations people interacting with other real people inside and outside of organizations.

❖ SYSTEMS ONLINE

You may not be able to judge a book by its cover, but you can learn a lot about an organization by its Web site. Some site designers build their Web sites for all their major publics. Others seem to cater exclusively to certain groups such as customers or stockholders. Looking at a college or university home page, you are likely to find links to entire sections of the Web site for students, prospective students, faculty and

16   PUBLIC RELATIONS ONLINE

staff, alumni, sports fans, the media, and library users among others. This makes it easy to identify the school's major publics.

An airline's home page, on the other hand, may be dominated by links for customers. Go ahead and book a flight from Moscow to Tokyo and order a window seat, but if you're an airplane food vendor, investigative reporter, or airline retiree seeking benefits information, you will have a harder time finding what you're looking for. If you are doing a report on an airline's competitive business strategy or how they have handled plane crashes, you might not find much at all. This doesn't mean the information isn't there, just that it is not accessible to everyone who stumbles on the main homepage. For example, until June 2004, American Airlines hosted two major Web sites for external publics—www.aa.com and www.AMRCorp.com. The first site is the one most of us would find via a search engine or list of travel links. The second site was designed for media and financial publics (who probably wouldn't be looking to book flights). News releases, corporate fact sheets, and financial information were available on www.AMRCorp.com. In 2004, AMRCorp.com was integrated into aa.com "in the interest of making public information about AMR Corporation, American Airlines, American Eagle Airlines, and other AMR entities available in the same location" ("AMRCorp.com," 2004). In any case, the Web site is a 24-hour-a-day, seven-day-a-week public communications tool, so naturally site designers might be reluctant to post information that gives away trade secrets, personnel information, or anything that gives visitors a negative impression.

In other words, not all online media need be available to all external publics. Following September 11, 2001, American Airlines used its employee intranet to communicate sensitive information during a time of tremendous environmental and legal constraints (Downing, 2004). Intranets use the same basic technical protocols as the Internet at large, but intranets can only be accessed with permission. Internet networks such as Web sites and intranets represent the systems in which public relations people work. The Internet at large represents the ever-changing environment in which network systems operate.

❖   WHAT MAKES A SYSTEM?

Systems are sets of interrelated parts, or objects. Systems theorists look at how the objects are related to each other, how the whole system differs from the sum of its parts, and how the system interacts with its environment. To understand what systems theory means for online public relations, we should first explore some of the key concepts.

Hierarchy. *Subsystems* are embedded in *suprasystems.* A university is a suprasystem that includes several subsystems: academic departments, student organizations, administrative offices, and so forth. The university Web page links to pages representing major subsystems. If you click on "academic departments" on a typical university Web site, you will find links to the colleges and schools that are subsystems. You will also find that the colleges are not just subsystems of the university, but that they're also suprasystems for departments such as public relations, advertising, and journalism.

Thanks mostly to Tim Berners-Lee, who is credited for inventing the World Wide Web, we don't have to start at the top of a hierarchy and work down every time we want to find information on the Internet. His invention helps computers work more like natural systems such as the human mind:

> A computer typically keeps information in rigid hierarchies and matrices, whereas the human mind has the special ability to link random bits of data. When I smell coffee, strong and stale, I may find myself again in a small room over a corner coffeehouse in Oxford. My brain makes a link, and instantly transports me there. (Berners-Lee & Fischetti, 1999, p. 3)

When computers make these seemingly random, but human-designed connections, we call it *hyperlinking.* Of course, search engines on the Web help too, but the concept of hyperlinking shows how systems are usually linked to each other in ways beside strict hierarchies.

Boundaries. Defining boundaries helps us identify the systems we wish to examine separate from the environments in which systems live. Domain names could work for this purpose. For instance, if we were examining American Airlines' Web site, we might say that any Web page that starts its URL with www.aa.com in the United States or any of American's other domains, such as www.aal.co.jp in Japan, count as *internal* to the system and anything else counts as *external.* This allows us to look at how systems communicate by accepting input from the external environment, including all suprasystems. If you go to the American Web site, fill out an online reservations request (don't forget the window seat), and hit submit, you are giving American Airlines input. After your request is processed (sometimes called *throughput*), your electronic ticket is issued, and that's *output.* In a very basic sense, this exchange is communication between a system and its environment.

Homeostasis. Have you ever heard the saying, "The more things change, the more they stay the same?" This is the basic paradox of

18   PUBLIC RELATIONS ONLINE

homeostasis. *Open systems* communicate well with their environment. They accept input and adapt to changes in the environment. They change their output as well, which affects the environment, which in turn has an effect back on the system. This cycle of adaptation is the essence of an open system. Yet all this change is a necessary part of an effort to remain stable. As Littlejohn (2002) puts it, "The open system is oriented toward life and growth," whereas *closed systems* move "toward chaos, disintegration and death" (p. 37). These outlooks for open versus closed systems represent the extremes, so we are better off thinking of systems as ranging on a continuum from relatively closed to relatively open. Homeostasis is the overall stability of more open systems, which is achieved via self-regulation and adaptability.

Cybernetics. Cybernetics, introduced by MIT mathematician Norbert Wiener (1961) in the 1940s and 1950s, is the study of communication, feedback, and control in goal-directed systems (Heylighen, 1997). *Control* and *self-regulation* are important concepts in cybernetics. Cybernetic systems exercise varying amounts of control in goal seeking by monitoring feedback.

Businesses and nonprofits that refuse to actually change themselves, simply trying to talk their way out of uncomfortable situations, operate more on the closed-system end of the spectrum. By not adapting to the environment, they set themselves up for failure. The public relations practitioner who cannot effect change in her own organization basically operates with her hands tied. It takes much more than just putting a positive spin on an event to help an organization adapt to its environment. If the goal of the organization is to remain competitive in business, fundraising, politics, or social activism, internal change and adaptation are absolutely necessary for success.

Purposeful activity. Ludwig von Bertalanffy (1968), the biologist who first proposed general systems theory, and the person from whom I borrowed the title of this chapter, emphasized the goal-directed nature of systems. We are going to continue under the assumption that good, strategic public relations are purposeful and goal-directed. With this in mind, we will shift our focus from online media as systems representing organizations to online media as tools used by real people trying to achieve goals and objectives within the context of organizations.

❖ PUTTING THE SYSTEMS VOCABULARY TO WORK

While the online reservations system at an airline automatically takes orders (input) and issues tickets (output), a real human might be monitoring the whole process to maintain homeostasis (although

I doubt this real human would spend much time talking to friends about "maintaining homeostasis"). If she sees a spike in the number of requests for organic meals, she might take that input and try to learn what kind of changes in the environment are causing the requests. After some research on diet trends, she might check with others at the airline who have contact with the airline's external publics—in this case, the external publics are customers.

Now suppose our airline employee learns that flight attendants are handling many onboard requests for organic meals, especially among business travelers. (This example makes the risky assumption that U.S. airlines will even serve food at all anymore by the time you read this.) Working toward a general goal of retaining or increasing the airline's market share of business travelers, she recommends to upper management that organic meals be offered to all passengers at check-in. This means that the airline must actually change the way it handles special-meal requests. After a trial run of the program and research on customer satisfaction (i.e., getting feedback), the airline's management learns that travelers like the service. They begin including mention of the service in their advertising and in the confirmation e-mails they send to customers who have just purchased tickets. They also pitch the story about their new service to health and fitness magazines, TV shows, and online forums for vegetarians. Media coverage is analyzed and more passenger feedback is then solicited to see how well the program is working, if at all. Perhaps organic meals become even more of a factor in consumer ticket purchasing decisions as a result.

This is an example of cybernetics in public relations. Someone working for an organization senses environmental pressure from both online and in-person sources. She recommends changes in the way the company does business. The organization adapts, and the changes are then communicated back into the environment. Feedback is continually monitored in an effort to achieve a longstanding goal to remain competitive in the business traveler market. Sound far-flung?

During a 2004 trend in low-carb dieting, a simple keyword search for *airline* and *low-carb meals* yielded a chart that compared major airlines in terms of their meal options and how much advanced notice was required to order special meals. (In case you're wondering, they ranged from 6 hours to 24 hours.) Airlines offering low-carb meals were featured in bold text with a friendly little airplane logo. The page's purpose?

Trying to get the message across to national and international service providers that low-carbohydrate eating plans are an important consideration to a large part of their clientele can be difficult. From restaurants to airlines to caterers, those that serve us our meals as we go about our daily routines need to learn to offer us the same allowances that they've been serving up to the low-fat crowd for years now. As you'll see below, some airlines are already taking the hint. I want you to be aware of them because those airlines that have listened to us deserve our business and the others need to keep hearing the message. When you fly, ask ahead of time for a low-carb meal option. Let them know this is imperative for you! ("Low-Carb Friendly," 2004)

What were the actual costs of providing low-carb meals? Would it have made sense to provide the meals with less than 24 hours notice, if at all? These would have been important management questions for public relations professionals to be involved in. It is also important to keep in mind that the low-carb crowd, as well as the "low-fat crowd," was a group that was practicing their own public relations. Just as the airline sites are public relations tools, so are sites such as www .lowcarbluxury.com.

A year later, a *Washington Post* story reported that the fad had faded (Pressler, 2005). One study showed that in 2004, 9.1% of Americans said they were on the low-carb tip. In 2005, that statistic was 2.2%. According to the article, many businesses that had catered to the vanishing low-carb crowd had quickly changed their course (Pressler, 2005). Such is the changing nature of marketplace environments, which require constant communication, monitoring, and adaptation for long-term success.

❖ SYSTEMS, ONLINE MEDIA, AND THE DAY-TO-DAY ROLES OF PUBLIC RELATIONS PEOPLE

Many of the terms we commonly use to identify excellence in public relations make clear sense in the context of systems theory. Let's consider the implications of online media for these common public relations role concepts.

Boundary spanning. Lots of people who work for organizations, such as ticket agents at airlines, work at the boundaries between organizations and their publics. But public relations people are uniquely positioned by their very job titles to support an interactive process of communication at these various points of contact. This is sometimes called the boundary-spanning role of public relations.

In discussing hierarchies, Koestler (1967) elicited the Roman god Janus to describe the dual faces of system boundaries. Janus, the god of gateways and doors, was depicted with two faces looking in opposite directions. Boundary spanners simultaneously face out to the environment and suprasystems and in toward the internal system and subsystems. Likewise, public relations people are often tasked with *informational boundary spanning*, which means collecting and interpreting environmental information, and *representational boundary spanning*, which means interpreting an organization's internal workings to those outside the system (Leichty & Springston, 1996).

With the boundary-spanning role in mind, and after a particularly frustrating online search for a campus parking map to send to a guest speaker at the University of Hawai'i, I had a brilliant idea. I ran down the hall to share it with fellow professor and new media design expert, Colin Macdonald. The University of Hawai'i, I explained, should design its Web site exactly like its organizational flow chart. That way the complex organization would be completely transparent to everyone. Macdonald just laughed.

The University of Hawai'i, like most organizations its size, is really complex. He asked me to imagine how hard it would be to find the parking Web page if I had to first learn the whole hierarchical structure of the flow chart that traced "Parking & Transportation Services" up to the university's board of regents.

He was right. New media should be designed with the users in mind. Representational boundary spanning means representing the organization to publics in ways *they* find useful—making complex internal workings easy to use for those outside the system.

Macdonald then pointed out that the parking page was readily available at www.hawaii.edu/parking/. Pretty tricky, huh? After getting over the minor ego embarrassment, I came away from that conversation with a new appreciation for the challenge of the online boundary-spanning role.

Managers, technicians, internals, and externals. Some public relations theorists have found it useful to distinguish between *manager* and *technician* roles in describing the day-to-day function of public relations people in organizations. "Managers make policy decisions and are held accountable for public relations program outcomes," whereas "technicians carry out the low-level mechanics of generating communication products that implement policy decisions made by others" (Dozier, 1992, p. 333). It's useful to think of these concepts along a continuum, with some public relations people practicing more of a manager role and others more of a technical role. It's unlikely that many practitioners fit exclusively into one of these categories.

Several scholars have elaborated these roles further. In fact, the overlapping roles of public relations people can also include *internals* or *externals*. Internals, like managers, counsel an organization's management, make communication policy decisions and coordinate internal public relations efforts. Externals represent their organizations to external publics, advocate for the organization, conduct research, and generally play an active role as the "public face" of their organizations (Leichty & Springston, 1996; Porter & Sallot, 2003). Again, the roles of internals and externals are not mutually exclusive.

Porter, Sallot, Cameron, and Shamp (2001) surveyed public relations practitioners to see if and how they were making use of fee-based online databases such as Lexis/Nexis and Dow Jones News Retrieval as well as Web engines like Yahoo and InfoSeek. They found that those who were using these online resources were more likely to report involvement in managerial decision making. They also found that online database use "improved two-way communications between internal and external environments, thereby increasing manager role enactment in public relations" (Porter et al., 2001, p. 182).

A few years later, Porter and Sallot (2003) followed up with a national e-mail survey of U.S. public relations people (mostly Public Relations Society of America members). The survey focused on Web use. They found the following:

1. Managers use the Web more than technicians for research and evaluation activities.

2. Managers use the Web more than technicians for "productivity and efficiency," including tasks such as preparing for public relations campaigns, monitoring the news, and identifying issues.

3. Technicians scored highest in activities such as two-way communication, monitoring online communities, communicating in online communities, and using Web traffic to show public relations results.

Although going online may at times seem more like a "technical" activity, recent research shows that online media are important in the functions of all public relations people, especially as they span the boundaries between their organizations and the environment.

In short, Janus, who could do it all, would make a fine public relations person. Most public relations people serve overlapping roles. Someone charged with managing an employee listserv or intranet will very likely work to keep the internal channels (and the decisions made there) up to date with outside news. And a media relations expert who primarily manages an organization's online pressroom and news distribution efforts will be wise to stay in touch with buzz in the organization by keeping up with intranet content, employee blogs, and so forth.

Proactive and reactive strategies. As Cutlip, Center, and Broom (2000) pointed out in *Effective Public Relations,* relatively closed systems are likely to react to the environment only after external pressure has reached the point at which it can no longer be ignored. Maybe today you can ignore those organic dieters, environmental protestors, budget-conscious students, or thrifty business competitors. But what if your organization starts losing passengers, community allies, students, or customers as a result of ignoring issues until they become crises? Your public relations options become fewer, and your work becomes more damage control than effective management of relationships between your organization and its publics. Public relations people operating in more-open systems actively monitor the environment for positive opportunities as well as potentially negative issues. This allows them to play a larger role in the organization's overall management, effecting change in the organization while the outcomes can be more about positive change (adaptation) than trying to control the chaos that characterizes crises. As we've learned from cybernetics, self-regulation is how systems manage to thrive in changing environments. But being proactive requires knowledge of what's going on in the environment.

The four-step process. A common approach to public relations work is to think of it as a four-step process: (1) research, (2) planning, (3) action and communication, and (4) evaluation. Note the cyclical, systemic nature of the process. *Research* gathers information from internal and external sources. *Planning* means deriving objectives from organizational goals. Purposive *action and communication* strategies are developed to meet these goals. And *evaluation* is used to get feedback and determine the effects of our efforts. In many cases, the evaluation of one effort is the foundation of further efforts.

Questionable Claims

It's All "Pull" Media Now!

Systems theory can be complicated. It is like trying to get a handle on the whole chicken-or-egg question. We all find it easier to process more straightforward claims, such as E. W. Brody's (2004) statement that "the supply-push age has ended and the demand-pull era has begun" (p. 8). But we might be better off looking at this statement as a fitting point of departure for discussing online media in public relations than as a declaration of fact.

Push media are media that push content to us as consumers of information. *War of the Worlds* was pushed into America's living rooms. No pay-perview back then. Today if you want to listen to the broadcast, you might go online and pull down an audio file. If you don't like what Bill O'Reilly has to say about Hillary Clinton, you can go to the Web, Internet radio, or another cable channel on your desktop computer and pull an entirely different perspective. Think of what this means for public relations. Rather than pushing information with news releases and public service announcements, public relations people have to find ways to convince people to actively seek their information. As Brody (2004) points out, cultivating loyalty and long-term relationships with publics is a big part of the job.

So is the text in your hand right now "push" or "pull?" If you're a student reading this as assigned reading, your answer might be, "It depends."

What about podcasting? This technology must be demand-pull-era media, right? But again, it depends.

You may find that getting into a good book means that you to go to a bricks-and-mortar bookstore or library and literally pull something from the shelves. On the other hand, some people use podcasts to be surprised by what turns up on news and music programs making podcasts more "push."

So whether the media are push or pull may have less to do with the era in which they were developed than with the uses people make of them and the gratifications they seek from these media. Building on the work of Cantril and Lazarsfeld and other early mass communication researchers who realized that audiences are more than just passive masses (see Chapter 1), uses-and-gratifications research became prominent in the late 1950s and early 1960s. Doing research to understand and anticipate the uses and gratifications sought by those choosing online media to communicate with an organization is an important step in effective online public relations. You'd interact differently—perhaps with different communication tools—with someone seeking to purchase an airline ticket than with someone seeking to write a report about the airline's safety record.

Systems, push, pull, loyalty, relationships, uses, and gratifications—these are lasting concepts that help us make sense of changing media. The answers are not always simple, but good theory and research help us avoid jumping to conclusions without considering context. This explains why scientists are so fond of their dependent and independent variables. Good theory helps us fill in the blank after "It depends on. . . . "

❖ WHY SYSTEMS THEORY MATTERS FOR ONLINE PUBLIC RELATIONS (AND WHY WE NEED OTHER THEORIES, TOO)

As we learned in Chapter 1, to be useful, knowledge about online public relations must be taken in context. The most important information in this chapter is not that public relations practitioners in the 1990s used

Lexis/Nexis and InfoSeek as databases. It's not the online presence of low-carb dieters. Nor is it the URL for parking maps of the University of Hawai'i. Communication technologies, online communities, and URLs change much too fast to be considered lasting concepts.

The more lasting concepts are ideas such as cybernetics, feedback, self-regulation and control, boundary spanning, and the cyclical public relations process. These concepts put the day-to-day practice of online public relations in a meaningful context.

These concepts matter because public relations practitioners must see how they are a large part of the human element that is so important in the way their employers interact with real people in the online environment. Although computer systems operate online 24 hours a day, seven days a week, and although organizations have come to depend on online systems for much of their day-to-day business, we must remember that computer systems are the technological tools of real people.

In the study of public relations—online or otherwise—we are mostly concerned with communication among these real people. I consider it poor customer relations when the computer system is blamed for my lost order, as if a person couldn't possibly be held accountable. Although Web sites, intranets, and relational databases lend themselves to systems-based design, the ones that are used for public relations purposes must work with us living, breathing people as well as they work with each other.

Systems theory alone isn't enough to make an organization's online Web presence a success in terms of public relations. Whereas systems theory helps us understand the technological tools of online public relations, and it puts our work in and among organizations in context, we need other theories of human communication to better understand how individuals communicate online. The next few chapters cover other ways of thinking about how public relations people use online media as tools in the interactive process of identifying, building, and maintaining relationships between organizations and publics.

❖ REFERENCES

AMRCorp.com information migrates to AA.com. (2004, June 24). Retrieved July 27, 2004, from http://www.amrcorp.com/

Berners-Lee, T., & Fischetti, M. (1999). *Weaving the Web: The original design and ultimate destiny of the World Wide Web by its inventor.* San Francisco: HarperSanFrancisco.

Bertalanffy, L. von. (1968). *General system theory: Foundations, development, applications.* New York: George Braziller.

Brody, E. W. (2004). Have you made the transition? Are you practicing public relations in the 21st century rather than the 20th? *Public Relations Quarterly, 49*(1), 7–9.

Cutlip, S. M., Center, A. H., & Broom, G. H. (2000). *Effective public relations* (8th ed.). Upper Saddle River, NJ: Prentice Hall.

Downing, J. R. (2004). American Airlines' use of mediated employee channels after the 9/11 attacks. *Public Relations Review, 30*, 37–48.

Dozier, D. M. (1992). The organizational roles of communications and public relations practitioners. In J. E. Grunig (Ed.), *Excellence in public relations and communication management* (pp. 327–356). Hillsdale, NJ: Lawrence Erlbaum Associates.

Heylighen, F. (1997). Cybernetics. In F. Heylighen, C. Joslyn, & V. Turchin (Eds.), *Principia cybernetica web*. Principia Cybernetica: Brussels. Retrieved June 7, 2006, from http://pespmc1.vub.ac.be/CYBERN.html

Koestler, A. (1967). *The ghost in the machine*. New York: Macmillan.

Leichty, G., & Springston, J. H. (1996). Elaborating public relations roles. *Public Relations Review, 73*, 467–477.

Littlejohn, S. W. (2002). *Theories of human communication* (7th ed.). Belmont, CA: Wadsworth/Thomson Learning.

Low-carb friendly. . . . Airline meals. (2004). Retrieved June 7, 2006, from http://www.lowcarbluxury.com/airlinefood.html

Porter, L. V., & Sallot, L. M. (2003). The Internet and public relations: Investigating practitioners' roles and World Wide Web use. *Journalism & Mass Communication Quarterly, 80*, 603–622.

Porter, L. V., Sallot, L. M., Cameron, G. T., & Shamp, S. (2001). New technologies and public relations: Exploring practitioners' use of online resources to earn a seat at the management table. *Journalism & Mass Communication Quarterly, 78*, 172–190.

Pressler, M. W. (2005, August 2). Low-carb fad fades, and Atkins is big loser. *Washington Post*, p. A01. Retrieved June 7, 2006, from http://www.washingtonpost.com/wpdyn/content/article/2005/08/02/AR2005080200276.html

Wiener, N. (1961). *Cybernetics* (2nd ed.). New York: John Wiley & Sons.

Systems Everywhere   27

Hands-Online Activity

❖ LINKING SYSTEMS

1. Find a Web page for a local nonprofit organization or for your own school. Make sure you pick a page that has plenty of links to other Web sites.

Name of Web page: _____

2. Name two different organizations that can be reached within one click of the home page (or two clicks if necessary).

Organization 1: _____

Organization 2: _____

3. Discuss:

a. Would you say these organizations are subsystems, suprasystems, or separate systems altogether in relation to the nonprofit or school you started with?

b. In what major ways, if any, might the linked systems have an effect on the nonprofit or school you chose?

c. In what major ways, if any, might your organization have an effect on these other systems?

28   PUBLIC RELATIONS ONLINE

     d. In which cases, if any, do you think a public relations person should be in charge of managing the communication between the systems? Why or why not?

3

Server-Side Public Relations

First we thought the PC was a calculator. Then we found out how to turn numbers into letters with ASCII—and we thought it was a typewriter. Then we discovered graphics, and we thought it was a television. With the World Wide Web, we've realized it's a brochure.

—Attributed to Douglas Adams
(Original source unknown)

❖ OVERVIEW

Public relations models and public relations practitioner typologies are presented to illustrate how online public relations can be practiced with a primarily "server-side" view. Then more specific communication tactics such as gathering, packaging, and disseminating information are discussed. Even primarily one-way tactics can be used to support interactive relationships between organizations and publics.

30   PUBLIC RELATIONS ONLINE

❖ SERVER-SIDE PUBLIC RELATIONS

Think about what a computer server does. If an organization hosts a Web site, what it really offers to people who visit the Web site is a bunch of data, computer memory, and processing power. These resources are housed on the organization's servers. When you type in www.yahoo .com or www.census.gov, you get access to all sorts of data, memory (disk space), and processing power. You might customize your census inquiry by seeking the numbers of native Hawaiian and Pacific Islanders in the state where your organization is recruiting new members, or you might just want to check your e-mail on your Yahoo account, but either way, your computer, referred to as a "client" in the client-server model of computing, requests help from the server.

Internal publics use server-side technology too. If you're a college student, you probably have e-mail on the college server. If you work in an office and work with large databases, chances are the data is saved (or at least backed up) on a server separate from the machine in front of you at your desk.

Just as computer networks can be seen as models of the social systems of public relations as well as tools for the practice of online public relations, client-server network architecture can be used to illustrate general approaches to online public relations. Although a server indeed "serves" information to other computers, the server holds most of the resources. The server-client relationship certainly involves two-way communication, but the greater balance of the relationship implies a more one-way process in which most information flows from the server to the desktops, laptops, media players, printers, and handheld devices of those receiving that information.

❖ ONE-WAY APPROACHES TO
ONLINE PUBLIC RELATIONS

James Grunig and Todd Hunt's (1984) models of public relations have been the target of much critical review and revision, but these models offer a useful framework for studying how public relations has been, and continues to be, practiced. Two of these models describe primarily one-way approaches, meaning that most the information flows from the organization as a source to publics as receivers in much the same way that data in a client-server connection flows from the server to clients.

Publicity and press agentry. Here, public relations people are most concerned with getting attention. Apple Computer, Inc., is famous for its publicity efforts to launch new products, dating back to 1984 when Apple introduced their Macintosh computer with a high-impact Super Bowl ad proclaiming, "On January 24th, Apple Computer will introduce the Macintosh. And you'll see why 1984 won't be like '1984.'" In a paper on the Apple advertisement and its place in the cultural history of computers, communication professor Ted Friedman (1997) described how the ad generated "mountains of extra free publicity" and helped secure Apple's American mindshare on the concept of personal computing (not to mention soaring stock values in the years that followed).

Yet America saw plenty of technology startups with mounds of publicity flop during the dot-com boom and bust in the late 1990s and early 2000s. Investors were so caught up in the hype that they lost sight of fundamental business principles. Lots of media attention translated into increased stock sales for a while, but eventually it became apparent that media attention alone wouldn't pay dividends. When dot-com startups failed to turn profits, and when the tech bubble burst, speculative investors were disappointed to realize that they had bought into hype, not substance. In the end, many businesses that shined on cleverly designed Web sites and in 30-second Super Bowl ads had little to offer when it came to substantial exchanges of resources.

The contrast between Apple's successes with publicity and the failure of so many dot-coms illustrates how publicity can be used as an effective tactic to support an organization's larger mission, but publicity alone doesn't guarantee success.

Public information. Chris Barnett, co-founder of the media relations newsletter *Bulldog Reporter,* put it this way in 2001 following the dot-com bust:

> Bottom line: Web sites with genuine news are a tremendous informational source for the consumer. However, as high priority publicity vehicles, they've run out of gas. (p. 33)

What separates the public information model from the publicity and press agentry model is an emphasis on accuracy and utility. Genuine news and valid information are the coins of trade for those in the business of public information. Think of all the layers of information available from www.census.gov. Resources range from population clocks on the main U.S. Census Bureau home page that show current estimates of the total U.S. and world population numbers to sophisticated analytical tools such as customizable data maps that allow users to see geographical population patterns based on recent census data. Of course, the census site also includes a newsroom with news releases,

32   PUBLIC RELATIONS ONLINE

fact sheets, and broadcast and photo resources. The U.S. Census Bureau was never able to make this much information so easily available to so many before the Internet. Any end user working with a client computer can gather and analyze a mind-boggling amount of information from the census servers. Likewise, organizations of all types—government agencies, nongovernmental organizations, nonprofits, blue-chip corporations, and home businesses—can use computer servers to provide information to publics without breaking their budgets on staffing, production, printing, and postage costs.

In fact, there is so much public information online that it can be really hard to make use of it without some careful attention to source credibility and search strategies. Both sending and receiving accurate information, then, are important skills for those practicing professional communication online.

❖ PRACTITIONER TYPOLOGIES

Another way of looking at what public relations people do online is to consider typologies. *Typologies* are categories for classifying and analyzing concepts. In this case, the lasting concepts are the roles of public relations people. Betteke van Ruler (2004) started with the Grunig and Hunt models, then reviewed some 50 years of literature relevant to the field of "communication management" (p. 125). *Communication management* is generally used in Europe to describe what would be called public relations in the United States. She also compared theory to professional perspectives of the field and found several typologies that describe what communication managers and public relations people do.

The town crier. van Ruler's (2004) town crier makes announcements for his organization but is limited to sending information about decisions that already have been made. "Segmentation of target groups is no problem, since town criers have a list in their computers of groups or individuals they want to reach" (p. 130).

The steward.[1] This typology highlights the pampering function of public relations. The steward makes sure that an organization's doors remain open. Keep in mind that open doors do not mean open systems. Mingling and socializing are a big part of her job. When I landed my first internship, I had never had a class in public relations. I asked my roommate what he thought I'd be doing. "Probably hosting cocktail parties and stuff like that," he said. He was picturing the steward type.

In 1994, one of the first examples of broad-scale consumer public relations on the Web was the MGD Tap Room, a site hosted by Miller

Genuine Draft to "tap into what's brewing on the lifestyle scene" (PRNewswire, 1994). It was worth a try, but hosting cocktail parties on a computer server is a pretty tall order.

The traffic manager. The traffic manager takes a more professional approach to communication. He focuses on strategic targeting, timing, and distribution of information. Although more sophisticated than the town crier and steward types, the traffic manager's claim to fame is still primarily one-way communication. He researches clips of stories placed in news media and sometimes measures audience recall of these stories or their key messages.

You may have received e-mails from organizations you belong to that highlight all the media "placements" the organizations have garnered. Most of these mentions can be retrieved online. Newspaper and magazine articles that run in print media generally have counterparts online, although the online version of the stories can be updated as new information emerges. Broadcast transcripts are available online, often for a small fee. And, of course, many placements are in media that are published exclusively online. The traffic manager sees the placement of each story as evidence of effectiveness. Getting the right message to the right audience at the right time is key, but without measuring more than recall, he must depend on his intuition and experience to gauge how effective his communication efforts are in terms of public response.

The conductor. The conductor harmonizes her organization's communication performance. The conductor moves her audience by leading all the instruments of communication with the same score. The score itself is written by the organization's top managers, who decide how they would like the organization to be positioned in the minds of its audiences and publics. The conductor, who also operates from the organization's upper echelons, orchestrates communication to fulfill the goals of positioning. This brings to mind the idea of integrated communication, in which all of an organization's communication functions—marketing, advertising, and public relations—work in sync, to speak in a single voice. Although the concept of integrated communication has been around for longer than the commercial uses of the Internet, it has been illustrated more vividly in recent years as online media converge with traditional communication channels, and the lines between advertising, marketing, and public relations become blurrier. For example, is an organization's Webmaster a public relations person? Or is she a marketing person? Or is she better characterized as an information manager? Or maybe even a communication manager? Regardless of title, this person is most likely concerned with the consistency of an organization's image on the Web. Furthermore, she

34   PUBLIC RELATIONS ONLINE

might report to someone who makes sure that information posted on the Web site is consistent with information going out via all the organization's other channels. This is the conductor type in action.

❖ GATHERING, PACKAGING, DISSEMINATING

Dot-com press agentry, online public information, database-driven town criers, virtual cocktail parties, digital traffic managers, and semiconductor symphonies; aren't these all just the traditional one-way functions of public relations taken into new media?

In many ways, yes. In his chapter entitled "Cyberspin," which focused on emerging communication technologies at the turn of the millennium, Edward Lordan (2001) suggested, "Regardless of the complexity and haphazard evolution of these technologies, they still are used primarily to gather, package and disseminate information" (p. 584).

Information gathering. Although gathering information is certainly in line with applied research conducted as part of two-way models of public relations and is an essential step in the cyclical four-step process of public relations, Lordan (2001) also suggested that computer technology is helping practitioners like the town crier target their one-way communication.

Databases in particular have been a big source for practitioner optimism about computers in public relations work. The Internet itself can be seen as one huge database. But just as a well-stocked rolodex of a few dozen personal contacts is often more useful than a million-person list of names and numbers in the white pages, an organizational database that includes data on people important to the organization will be more useful than the results of general Web queries.

For example, a university relations executive might keep a database of alumni, donors, state legislators, students, faculty, football season ticket holders, and so forth. Basic information on each person can be gathered at every opportunity to build and maintain this list. If law and policy permit, the university relations executive might start with a list of graduating seniors provided by the registrar. Then she might enter the names of donors from an alumni association database. Online season ticket order forms might provide information from the school's athletic association that can be shared with the office of university relations, and so on.

Obviously building and maintaining such a database has become much easier with the evolution of computers and server-side technology. If you've never had to hand address (or hand type) a large batch of snail-mail, be thankful. Although generating mailing lists and mailing labels with a computer is standard practice now, you can probably understand why public relations people were so optimistic about the dawning of the digital age. Although a mailing list is still a mailing list, the effect of computers on the day-to-day work of professional communicators would be hard to overstate.

What is making database use in public relations more interesting is the growing use of relational databases in managing public relations work. Suppose our university relations director has learned that a prominent state legislator is planning to attend a tailgate social at homecoming. With a relational database, she can quickly generate a list of recent graduates who have donated money in the past year, who now live in the legislator's district, and who hold season football tickets. Then the people on this list can be invited to RSVP online. When the alumni-donor-constituent football fans sign in to the RSVP page hosted on a university server, they can be greeted with a personalized message and confirmation. What follows once the RSVPs are in may begin to look more like a two-way approach to public relations, but the idea of using databases to collect information on target publics highlights how even the one-way tactics of the town crier can be eased by information-gathering technology.

Questionable Claims

❖ THE INTERNET GREW FASTER
THAN ANY MEDIUM IN HISTORY!

In an overview of how public relations professionals were using emerging media in public relations for primarily one-way communication at the turn of the millennium, Lordan (2001) attributed the rapid adoption of new media in public relations to "unparalleled growth" in six related areas, including the amount of information available (p. 583). It would be hard to argue with Lordan that the nature of the Internet is much more information intensive than "traditional" media, but what about the growth of the Internet itself? Middleberg (2001), for example, offered public relations people some statistics that were hard to ignore, such as, "Seven people log on to the Internet for the first time every second" (p. 34). What other medium can touch that?

Kent (2001) cites FitzGerald and Spagnolia (1999) who cited an Associated Press article in the *Washington Post* that reported the following: "Internet traffic doubles every 100 days. While it took radio 38 years to establish 50 million listeners and television 13 years to attract 50 million viewers, in four years the Internet acquired 50 million users" (FitzGerald & Spagnolia, 1999, p. 12).

Hannemyr (2003) began to wonder about quotes like the following from a book called *Successful Cybermarketing in a Week*:

Cyberfact: It took 38 years for radio to attract 50 million listeners. 13 years for television to attract 50 million viewers. In just 4 years the Internet has attracted 50 million surfers! Those figures can hardly be balked at, especially when you consider the Internet's beginnings. (Gabay, 2000)

Sound familiar? Hannemyr (2003) thought so too, so he tried to chase down the actual sources of such information. He found that these quotes often have been attributed to as many as a dozen different sources, that they often lack specifics such as times and dates, and that the data are usually referenced to an individual person (e.g., "Bill Gates once said . . ."). He went on to seek the best statistics available on Internet usage in the United States, such as those from the U.S. Census Bureau. Realizing that there was no one "correct" data set, he consulted several sources, and more important, put the data in context and used theory to give it some meaning.

For instance, what does it mean that the Internet had an estimated 79 million U.S. users in 1999? Based on actor-network theory and diffusion theory, Hannemyr (2003) makes a fairly compelling argument that 1989 can be used as the "base" year of the Internet as a theoretically irreversible social phenomenon. This is when commercial Internet service providers went online and the Internet was no longer confined to military, academic, and scientific communities. We could say then that the Internet as we know it was 10 years old in 1999.

For radio, Hannemyr (2003) points to 1920 as a base year, when commercial broadcast radio was born, and shows that 10 years later, in 1930, an estimated 56 million people in the United States were radio users. For television, he argues that the base is 1945, when the post-war electronics industry began to produce televisions for large consumer markets. As a budding 10-year-old in 1955, television had about 80 million viewers in the United States. Compare that now to the Internet's 79 million U.S. users on its 10th birthday as a commercial medium. Driving the point even further, Hannemyr converts the estimated number of users to percentages of the population to calculate adoption rates. When the numbers are crunched like this, that figure of 79 million Internet users means an adoption rate of about 30%, whereas television's 80 million viewers in 1955 and radio's 56 million listeners in 1930 indicate adoption rates closer to 50%.

Information packaging. The conductor typology reminds us of the importance of information packaging in professional communication. Public relations people are often in charge of how an organization presents itself, and for this, public relations people are often criticized. Much of this criticism is aimed at "fluff," information presented to look or sound good that carries little substantive meaning. The advent of desktop publishing software and the Internet as an infinite source of graphics have made it possible for non-graphic-design people to produce their own brochures, newsletters, Web sites, and other materials that used to require the services of professional printers and graphic designers. The good news is that just about anyone with a computer can publish on behalf of his or her organization. The bad news is, well, that just about anyone with a computer can publish on behalf of his or her organization—with very little quality control.

Without clearly presented information, an organization will have a hard time communicating with its publics. Like a mumbling spokesperson or a news release with a typo in the headline, a Web page with poor graphic design and broken links usually will not win much third-party media coverage. Not only will news media seriously question the credibility of the poorly designed Web site, so will consumers, donors, investors, vendors, volunteers, and members of any other public who might come across it.

Depending on the function of your online communication efforts, you may need professional help. A small nonprofit organization may do just fine with online materials produced from the single desktop computer of a sharp public relations person. For example, a public relations person might produce a monthly newsletter that she e-mails to members, a basic Web site, online volunteer sign-up forms that are used to update a volunteer database and mailing list, and a CD-ROM or a DVD produced for potential donors that features the organization's mission and history. Each of these items will require basic skills in writing, editing, layout, and design.

On the other hand, a Fortune 500 company competing with other Fortune 500 companies will need a level of expertise in producing its online operations that far exceeds the skills of any one person. Specialists in Web design, video production, and database management among others will be needed to produce a quality online presence. This really isn't much different from pre-Internet media, in which a small organization can communicate with its local publics with mostly in-house resources, but the national and international communication efforts of large corporations require professional help from advertising agencies to produce spots suitable for global airing and publication. Making messages sound or look good is critical, but it isn't enough. Public relations people must see to it that the content of communication is meaningful and accurate.

Information dissemination. Much online public relations essentially consists of traditional tactics translated into new media. Many Web sites are basically online brochures, referred to as *brochureware*. E-mail messages with "To:," "From:," "CC:," and "Subject:" headings are online memos. Here are some other examples:

38   PUBLIC RELATIONS ONLINE

- **Online news releases.** Although these might include some features such as links to Web sites and more detailed background information, most e-mail news releases still serve the basic function of providing journalists with news about an organization. Actual news value and clear writing—what you learn in a news-writing course—are still the primary criteria for success. Targeting the right journalists for your news is also key, as it always has been. Without printing and postage costs, it might be tempting to blast your news releases out to the widest available distribution list available, but this strategy carries the risk of backfiring by just annoying receivers who will see your news as spam. Online media relations is an important part of online public relations.

- **E-zines and newsletters.** These are the electronic versions of magazines and newsletters, although the formatting decisions you make in writing and designing these publications are different online. For example, you must take into consideration each receiver's software capabilities. Many experts still advise sending e-mail newsletters in plain-text format. This is the only way to ensure that all your readers will get the basic information without graphic mishaps. Many readers have the capability to view e-mail in HTML and richer formats, but set their e-mail preferences to show only plain text. There are ways around this for the sender, like sending newsletters as attachments (e.g., as MS Word or PDF files) or sending receivers to your Web page to see your newsletter or magazine, but these require your receivers to be more than just receivers. They must be active information seekers who choose to take your material. However, as long as you treat e-zines and newsletters as push media, in which you push the information to receivers and hope that they take it, you are basically working with traditional information dissemination tactics.

- **Public service announcements (PSAs).** If e-mail, e-zines, and online newsletters are the digital versions of public relations' favorite print tactics, online PSAs, and to some degree, video news releases (VNRs), are their counterparts for broadcast media. Rather than sending analog audio and videotapes via UPS or FedEx, public relations practitioners can digitize their audio and video materials and send them over the ether. (FTP and Web downloads directly from the organization's server usually work better than e-mail for transferring big files, but it's still often more practical to just send a tape, CD, or DVD.) In any case, the underlying purpose of PSAs remains to support the overlapping interests of your organization and its external publics: wearing seatbelts, planting trees, saying no to drugs, and the like.

- **Streaming audio and video.** Whereas PSAs and VNRs are generally delivered as recorded materials, which are viewed, replayed, edited, and often trashed at the will of station producers, journalists, and anyone else with access to the digital files, streaming audio and video are the online versions of live radio and TV signals. Listeners and viewers hear and see the signal as it is sent from your server, rather than waiting for the entire file to download before playing it or editing it. From a consumer's perspective, streaming media really aren't any newer than traditional radio and TV. These media do, however, illustrate the concept of technological *convergence* of previously separate media channels. As consumer television begins to operate more like the Internet, with receivers gaining more control of what they see and when they see it (e.g., pausing and replaying "live" TV), and as the Internet begins to look more like TV, with audio and video broadband signals being delivered at a speed and quality more on par with cable, the distinction between online and traditional is less meaningful.

Although providing targeted, useful, and aesthetically pleasing information is still very much a key function of public relations work—it is necessary in the practice of public relations—it is not sufficient for successful public relations, or even successful publicity. Although online media allow professional communicators to bypass the editorial process often required in getting information out through traditional news outlets in print or broadcast media, the catch is that credibility still has to be earned, online or not. An article in *The Wall Street Journal Online* will still carry more weight with most readers than a news release posted on a Web site of an unknown company. Publicity stunts may get attention, but that doesn't mean they will build credibility. Psychologists have defined credibility as a function of both trustworthiness and expertise. Establishing trustworthiness and expertise in the minds of those with whom you communicate takes a lot more than just getting their attention.

❖ ONE-WAY TACTICS AND INTERACTIVE PUBLIC RELATIONS

E-mail news releases often lead to almost instant feedback from reporters, quickly becoming more an issue of interactive relationships with journalists than one-way dissemination of information (O'Keefe, 2002). Effective e-zines require both an understanding of user interests and technical capabilities. Online PSAs will sit untouched in cyberspace unless receivers see the benefit to someone besides the sender. Effective use of streaming media means understanding receivers as active people rather than clients

40   PUBLIC RELATIONS ONLINE

who retrieve information from an organization's servers. Real interactive public relations online depends on how people are using online media as tools to interact with organizations, even when the organization seems to hold most the resources involved in the exchange.

❖ NOTE

1. This definition of *steward* shouldn't be confused with Kathleen Kelly's (2001) concept of stewardship in fundraising, which suggests "Public relations practitioners are attentive to every aspect of the organization's behavior that might affect relations with supportive publics" (p. 284).

❖ REFERENCES

Barnett, C. (2001). Pitching "new media" today is largely a waste of time and money. *Public Relations Strategist, 8*(3), 30–34.

FitzGerald, S. S., & Spagnolia. N. (1999). Four predictions for PR practitioners in the new millennium. *Public Relations Quarterly, 44*(3), 12–15.

Friedman, T. (1997, October). *Apple's 1984: The introduction of the Macintosh in the cultural history of personal computers.* Paper presented at the Society for the History of Technology Convention, Pasadena, CA. Revised version retrieved June 8, 2006, from http://www.duke.edu/~tlove/mac.htm

Gabay, J. J. (2000). *Successful cybermarketing in a week.* London: Hodder & Stoughton.

Grunig, J. E., & Hunt, T. (1984). *Managing public relations.* New York: Holt, Rinehart and Winston.

Hannemyr, G. (2003). The Internet as hyperbole: A critical examination of adoption rates. *Information Society, 19*(2), 11–121. Retrieved June 8, 2006, from http://folk.uio.no/gisle/essay/diff.html

Kelly, K. (2001). Stewardship: The fifth step in the public relations process. In R. L. Heath (Ed.), *Handbook of public relations* (pp. 279–290). Thousand Oaks, CA: Sage.

Kent, Michael. L. (2001). Essential tips for searching the Web. *Public Relations Quarterly, 46*(1), 26–30.

Lordan, E. J. (2001). Cyberspin: The use of new technologies in public relations. In R. L. Heath (Ed.), *Handbook of public relations* (pp. 583–589). Thousand Oaks, CA: Sage.

Middleberg, D. (2001). *Winning PR in the wired world: Powerful communication strategies for the noisy digital space.* New York: McGraw-Hill.

O'Keefe, S. (2002). *Complete guide to Internet publicity: Creating and launching successful online campaigns.* New York: John Wiley & Sons.

PRNewswire. (1994, October 18).—*Burp—Miller Genuine Draft opens MGD tap room on the Web.* Retrieved June 8, 2006, from http://www.interesting-people .org/archives/interesting people/199410/msg00036.html

van Ruler, B. (2004). The communication grid: An introduction of a model of four communication strategies. *Public Relations Review, 30*, 123–143.

Server-Side Public Relations   41

Hands-Online Activity

❖ WHAT'S NEW IN ONLINE PUBLIC RELATIONS?

Suppose you work for *PRWeek* (http://www.prweek.com/), *PR Tactics* (http://www.prsa.org/_Publications/magazines/tactics.asp), or a similar public relations trade publication.

1. Find an online public relations tactic that would make for an interesting story for your readers—maybe a unique way of distributing news releases, a live video feed, a corporate blog, a PDA message delivery service, or an intranet feature that you have access to. Hint: If you use a search engine to find public relations blogs, you'll probably find some leads from public relations bloggers.

Tactic: _____

2. Write the first paragraph or two of your story to describe what's happening and what makes it worth reading about. If you are working in a class that has an online class discussion forum, this might be a good way to open new threads for discussion.

3. Discuss: Do any of the typologies or models discussed in this chapter offer a good fit for the tactic you describe? Which comes closest? Why does or doesn't this typology/model match the tactic well?

4

Peer-to-Peer Public Relations

In the age of the Web where hype blows up in your face and spin gets taken as an insult, the real work of PR will be more important than ever.

—Doc Searls and David Weinberger (2001, p. 90)

❖ OVERVIEW

Online media give us new options for practicing public relations with more of a peer-to-peer view of the communication process. This chapter covers parallel ranges of communication concepts: from asymmetrical to symmetrical, from denotative to connotative, from monologic to dialogic, and from seeing markets as targets to seeing markets as conversations. Online, where the relative balance of power between organizations and publics is shifting, understanding these concepts is critical to practicing smart public relations.

44   PUBLIC RELATIONS ONLINE

❖ PEER-TO-PEER PUBLIC RELATIONS

If you have ever used a file-sharing program like Kazaa, Limewire, WinMX, or Napster to download audio, video, or text files, then you have worked on a computer that could simultaneously function as both a server (providing files for others to download) and a client (downloading files from others). Now granted, when those shared files contain copyrighted material, the networks run into legal issues, which is what led to the downfall of Napster and WinMX, but the concept of people working in peer-to-peer networks in the legitimate and productive exchange of original resources is becoming more and more prevalent online. Yale law professor Yochai Benkler (2006) has suggested that the general characteristics of peer-to-peer networks are changing the very nature of "information production fields":

> The material requirements for effective information production and communication are now owned by numbers of individuals several orders of magnitude larger than the number of owners of the basic means of information production and exchange a mere two decades ago . . . . We are beginning to see the expansion of this model not only to our core software platforms, but beyond them into every domain of information and cultural production . . . from peer production of encyclopedias, to news and commentary, to immersive entertainment. (pp. 4–5)

Whereas computing power and digital resources are concentrated on servers in server-side online operations, peer-to-peer networks work with resources that are more evenly distributed among the participants. This potential for more balance in the communication process makes peer-to-peer technology a useful metaphor for online public relations.

Whereas public relations books and academic articles of the 1980s focused most often on tools and tips for one-way communication tactics such as publicity, corporate advertising, audiovisual techniques, and effects-based communication efforts, public relations scholarship in the new millennium is just as likely to cover symmetrical models of communication, women's studies, diversity, and negotiation (Botan & Taylor, 2004). But it's not just the thinking about public relations that has shifted, the online technologies of everyday public relations are allowing the practice of effective public relations more room to move from one-way message targeting to two-way conversations.

❖ TWO-WAY MODELS

Putting communication processes into neat little boxes with labels such as one-way and two-way can be tricky. If you define effective communication as a process that requires some sort of feedback, you might argue that all communication is two way, but even so, there is obviously a broad range in the way communication channels are used. An organization's intranet, for example, might be used simply for top corporate officers to make announcements to employees, who in turn acknowledge receiving the messages by showing up at the meetings announced or turning in downloaded forms on time. Or the exact same technology may be adopted by employees as an open forum to voice their new ideas, post news from the frontlines, and discuss candid concerns with organizational management. The online technology allows for two-way communication in either case, but the directional flow of influence varies enormously based on how people use it.

As discussed in Chapter 3, the Grunig and Hunt models of public relations represent basic ways that public relations people perceive their jobs in general. The publicity and press agentry model and the public information model are considered primarily one-way approaches to public relations. The two-way models that follow are distinguished based on symmetry, or balance, in the directional flow of influence between an organization and its publics.

Two-way asymmetrical public relations is unbalanced. In this model, an organization gets feedback from its publics but uses this feedback as a basis for trying to persuade the publics to change. A key underpinning of asymmetrical communication strategies is that an organization wants the people it communicates with to change in some way, but the organization is unlikely to change much itself.

Take for example Burson-Marsteller's work for Hewlett-Packard China's (HPC's) Imaging and Printing Group in China:

> HPC conducted market research targeting almost 12,000 consumers in China to ascertain their usage and behavioral attitudes towards digital imaging, with the objective of developing a marketing concept HPC could own for the launch. The research covered six cities including Beijing, Shanghai, Guangzhou, Chengdu, Shenzhen and Hangzhou, and targeted two audience groups—25- to 32-year-old affluent singles and couples, and 33- to 40-year-old couples with children. From the research, HPC concluded that consumers in China want to do more with what they have, as opposed to having

46   PUBLIC RELATIONS ONLINE

more features in their [information technology] products. (as cited in "Case Study," 2004)

With the results of this research, Burson-Marsteller (as cited in "Case Study," 2004) developed a campaign that combined online media with print and broadcast media to launch HP products with the theme, "At Home With HP: Out of This World." A highlight of the campaign was an online competition hosted on a major Chinese Internet portal called sina.com to recruit 99 families from across the country to try the HP products (PCs and all-in-one devices). More than 5,000 families entered the competition, which required them to submit pictures and family stories online. The families, and the trade media that covered the campaign activities, were used to "seed" the market prior to launching the HP products to the larger population. Of course, the 99 families and the trade media benefited with free HP products, but HP benefited with people to serve as seeds for their public relations–driven product launch. The feedback Burson-Marsteller and HP gathered from consumers was part of a two-way communication process, but the larger benefit Burson-Marsteller reportedly delivered was designed for HP.

Two-way asymmetrical tactics are not limited to sales-support public relations. Political strategists do a lot of research to learn which issues will resonate with key voting blocks before preparing their candidates to speak with these people. The main idea isn't as much to inform policy as it is to win votes (and raise funds). To the extent that the political candidate uses her political resources to control the "conversation," and to the extent that the public relations person promoting his client's new product uses his budget and media connections to get his key message across to masses of people, the balance of power favors the organization in the organization-public relationship. Both cases are asymmetrical.

Research and persuasion, online or otherwise, are not inherently bad or unethical. The political candidate and her advisors may be seeking to do very good things for their constituents if elected. They may even get voters more engaged in democratic processes if their arguments are engaging enough. The product promoter might be promoting healthy foods, which would benefit consumers in the long run. (Burson-Marsteller also develops campaigns to fight obesity.) When organizations begin to take publics' real interests into account and balance organizational interests with public interests, their strategies start to move toward the symmetrical end of the continuum.

Two-way symmetrical public relations then means (a) the organization takes the interests of publics into careful consideration, and (b) public relations practitioners seek some sort of balance between the interests of their organizations and the interests of publics. Interactive communication greatly enhances an organization's ability to practice symmetrical public relations.

In symmetrical public relations terms, *organization* and *public* are almost interchangeable. Of course, organizations usually communicate differently with different groups in different situations (Leichty & Springston, 1993). The exchange between HP and sina.com, for example, might have been more symmetrical, whereas the relationship between HP and consumers was more asymmetrical. Likewise, HP might have, at times, been open to suggestions from consumers on how the company actually designed and marketed products. In online environments, in which publics have much greater access to the channels of communication compared with traditional mass media environments, many publics are realizing more power in the communication process. Some have argued that the relatively low cost of getting online to deliver information and express opinions has put activists, government agencies, and corporations more "on par" online, and that the Internet is a "potential equalizer" (Coombs, 1998, p. 289; Heath, 1998, p. 273).

❖ TWO-WAY TYPOLOGIES

Betteke van Ruler (2004) suggests two two-way typologies for understanding what public relations people do. Rather than looking at the concept of symmetry to describe the range of two-way communication, she recommends we consider whether communication is more about denotative (information as "objective") or connotative (information as "subjective") meaning. You get denotative meaning by looking something up in a dictionary. The Internet, according to the *Merriam-Webster Online Dictionary* (n.d.), is "an electronic communications network that connects computer networks and organizational computer facilities around the world." That's denotative meaning. But whether you see the Internet as a playground, a giant library, a worldwide swap meet, a frightening underworld of lurking criminals, or some combination of all these is more a matter of connotative meaning. Connotative meaning according to van Ruler (2004), "refers to all personal feelings and subjective associations to a symbol" (p. 127).[1]

The creator. Van Ruler's (2004) creator typology describes a public relations person whose job it is "to create agreement between the organization, or its members, and its constituencies" (p. 135). The creator type aims for mutually beneficial relationships, cooperation, and common ground. Therefore, the creator aspires to somewhat symmetrical

48   PUBLIC RELATIONS ONLINE

communication. The meaning delivered by the creator is denotative. For example, Ogilvy Public Relations Worldwide worked with the Centers for Disease Control to develop kits designed to educate and train labor leaders and business managers to handle HIV/AIDS issues in the workplace:

> HIV/AIDS–related stigma and misinformation about the trans-mission of the virus was proving to be a contentious issue in offices and on unionized job sites. Businesses and unions, already pressed on insurance expenses and other health related issues, were reluctant to address HIV/AIDS directly. . . . An online pro-motional campaign focusing on the availability of the Manager's Kit and Labor Leader's Kit from the www.hivatwork.org Web site resulted in a 440 percent increase in downloads of the kit compo-nents in the first eight months. ("HIV at Work," 2005)

The kit tactic is a good example of using online media to dissemi-nate information more efficiently. The kits were composed of PDF files—a classic example of traditional text and graphics simply digi-tized for online distribution—but this one-way tactic was clearly part of a larger effort that used research to learn the concerns of business and labor leaders:

> From our field research, Ogilvy . . . learned that in order to be accepted by workers and staff, workplace education had to be endorsed and initiated by senior management and labor leaders. Only through their support and leadership would worker accep-tance be possible. ("HIV at Work," 2005)

So the larger communication strategy, which included field research, can be seen as two-way. Yet the terms *educate* and *train*, as listed in the description of the goals for the downloadable kits, suggest a transmission of denotative meaning. Those working at Ogilvy fit the creator typology in this example. They know what HIV/AIDS is and what they want to communicate about it. They seek to have their con-stituents understand and agree with this denotative meaning.

The facilitator. The facilitator sees her job as more of a dialogic communication process. Facilitator types focus more on connotative meaning. Although Ogilvy and their clients are in a good position to tell us what HIV/AIDS *is*, they would be hard pressed to post a PDF file telling us what the affliction *means* to those fighting it around the world. The International Community of Women Living With

HIV/AIDS (2005), on the other hand, "is honoured and proud to be the only international network which strives to share with the global community the experiences, views and contributions of 19 million incredible women worldwide, who are also HIV positive." The Web site, although not as slick as those produced for top clients of international public relations agencies, includes direct contact information and discussion forums for women around the world who share the organization's concerns. Any public relations efforts apparent on the page, however, are best represented by van Ruler's (2004) description of the facilitator's job: to "create environments in which meaningful dialogues can flourish" (p. 136).

Dialogue

All dialogue might involve two-way communication, but not all two-way communication is dialogue. When organizations practice two-way communications as simply means to an end, even if that end is socially beneficial, they aren't involved in a true dialogue. Doing research and getting feedback as part of a communications strategy is not really dialogue. Dialogue, as communication theorists have conceptualized it, is a heavily philosophical concept describing a process rather than an outcome (cf. Arnett, 1981; Buber, 1958). Public relations people might be involved with this kind of dialogue if and when they find themselves in a humanistic exchange of empathy with another. But this isn't really something you can put in your daily planner. If you did, you'd probably have to squeeze it in somewhere after lunch but before self-actualization.

This isn't to say that we cannot take some useful ideas away from the high theory of dialogue. In fact, Michael Kent and Maureen Taylor (1998) have used the concept of dialogue to identify smart uses of the Web in public relations. They point out that (a) dialogue doesn't mean agreement, and (b) dialogue is about intersubjectivity and not objective truth. For now, let's leave the true essence of dialogue with a capital "D" to the philosophers. Rather, let's hedge a little and use the term *dialogic communication* to describe communication when it is seen as a collaborative process of building connotative meaning as opposed to a functional process of delivering denotative meaning. A stagnant Web site, preprogrammed e-mail application, and even a voicemail system can do the latter: "For information on our products, press 3." Dialogic communication requires real people to get (and stay) involved in the conversation.

Kent and Taylor offered some down-to-earth principles of dialogic communication that have stood the test of time (at least in Web years—since 1998).

50   PUBLIC RELATIONS ONLINE

Dialogic loop. Organizations communicating online should let people get in touch to ask questions and voice concerns. That is the easy part. Almost every business, nonprofit, and interest group with a home page also has a "contact us" link posted somewhere. Whether, and how, they actually respond is the litmus test for real interactivity (i.e., contingency interactivity). I once ordered a pair of shoes online from a national retailer. The shoes never arrived. I went online and hit the "customer support" link, which took me to an online form that I had to fill out with the details of my order. (No phone number was posted.) Completing and submitting that form gave me a tracking number and link to the delivery service. The delivery service Web site did show my tracking number, and that a shipment of some sort had been made. But I still didn't have my shoes. I e-mailed customer service and received an automated response with a link back to the "customer support" page where I started. This is *not* a dialogic loop.

This story goes on and on with calls to the delivery service, an online visit to the retailer's corporate home page to get a phone number, and a maze of voicemail designed to make sure I didn't actually speak with a real person. Finally, when I did get in touch with another human, we had a really unsatisfying conversation about the status of my order. Nothing was resolved. A few weeks later, I saw that at least my payment had been credited back to my credit card account. I'll never try to buy anything from that company again. No shoes, no stock, no dice.

As Kent and Taylor (1998) put it, "Response is a major part of the dialogic loop, however, the content of the response is also critical for relationship building" (p. 327).

Usefulness of information. Providing useful information is an important part of one-way communication, but ensuring the usability of online communication requires a more two-way process of understanding what your publics are looking for (more on usability in Chapter 10). Useful information as a principle of dialogic communication means that you are providing publics something of substance that will allow them to engage you as informed partners.

Sure, the online shoe shop let me see all the styles, sizes, and colors. That was somewhat useful. The online shopping might even have been construed as two way and functionally interactive as I entered my preferences and saw the product pictures change and which items were on sale, but it was definitely not dialogic.

On the other hand, a quick Google search for the company's name and *customer service* turned up an independent customer-review-and-rating bulletin board ("BizRate," 2005). Of course, lots of customers

Peer-to-Peer Public Relations   51

(the ones who actually received their orders as expected) were happy with the retailer, but too many others shared my concerns. The following are the five posts made in the five days prior to my query. Never mind the broken English and the typos; I would have found the human voices on this page just as useful, if not more so, than the expertly designed shoe store home page:

• I bought some shoes from the [company] site. They were advertised as "soft upper," but when I received them they were very hard penny loafers. It also took quite a while for delivery and I could not find a way to track the shipment.

• was sent an email w/ the sale price on an item. check the website to place the order and the regular price was given to me. Checked w/ customer svc via phone and they didn't know anything about it. I had to check the website every couple of days for a week and half until the correct prices were posted.

• Local stores no longer carry Boat Shoes. Went on-line and had the product within 5 Days. Excellent service and a great fit.

• When I E-mail customer servive on the pair of shoes I wanted and didn't find on the Internet site. I E-mail them to find out if they where still avaible and if they where not, what would be there replacement. All they told me was they where no longer avaible. But didn't tell me what it replacement was. Very poor customer servive for someone who is saleing shoes. I had to call the Corperate Office to find the replacement

• please can you tell me where is my order please call me at . . .

The last comment made me wonder what the chances were that anyone would ever call the person back. Next time, I'll check the ratings page first.

Generating return visits. Dialogic communication means not just getting people engaged in a back-and-forth conversation, but also keeping them engaged. This is an area in which public relations differs somewhat from marketing.

Surprisingly, three of the five people cited above indicated that they "would shop here again," as noted with a little green smiley face next to their comments. In a marketing sense, this is a 60% success rate. When I think of myself as marketers think of me—as a customer—I see a successful online transaction as one in which I get on the Web, find what I need, buy it, and have it delivered in a minimal amount of time.

52   PUBLIC RELATIONS ONLINE

When my order goes through smoothly, I normally don't want to dialogue about the product (i.e., "What do shoes really *mean*?").

But members of customer publics are often existing or potential members of other publics—including journalists, stockholders, regulators, suppliers, employees, neighbors, and activists. Encouraging these people to become "return visitors" and not just "repeat customers" is a public relations function that means offering something of value beyond a marketable product. It means inviting them to get involved in a conversation. Journalists, stockholders, and regulators always have been likely to have their concerns taken seriously. Imagine treating a *Wall Street Journal* reporter or a Securities and Exchange Commission official like a customer: "Your feedback is important to us. Press one for a quote from our CEO. Press two for our response to auditors. Or remain on the line to hear these options again." Taking the same approach online with links to a stagnant "press room" or "investor relations" page with canned content is just as silly. An organization needs to offer something worth returning for if it wants to use online media to develop relationships with any of its publics. Keep in mind that employees, neighbors, and activists are organized online too. Online, the organization-public distinction is easily reversed.

Markets as Conversations—Another Perspective on "PR Types"

Doc Searls and David Weinberger are two of the Internet's most respected voices when it comes to understanding the shift in emphasis online from traditional marketing and public relations practices to approaches that give much greater weight to the voices of publics. And what do they think of "PR types?" "They're the used car salesmen of the corporate world," say Searls and Weinberger (2001). But then they write:

Of course, the best of the people in PR are not PR Types at all. They understand that they aren't censors, they're the company's best conversationalists. (p. 90)

Searls and Weinberger (2001) see online markets as conversations, not as targets. As they explain, the first markets were places where people gathered to do business and exchange ideas—a far cry from my online shoe store. These markets brought people with shared interests together to discuss wares and services. Buyers and sellers talked to each other in ways mass media would never allow. Business models of the late 20th century, however, were developed to deliver large shipments of uniform products to distant markets.

Advertisers, marketers, and public relations people followed suit in the only way that made sense for such mass markets. They sought to deliver their messages with mass communication. Strategic mass communication came to mean getting a persuasive message to work on a target market, and these target markets came to be defined based on their demographic, geographic, and even sociographic profiles. What riddles businesses now is how to stay in touch with these markets as the media used to communicate with them are de-massifying.

Searls and Weinberger (2001) recommend getting back to the concept of markets as conversations among peers, which means speaking with a human voice and getting away from the tactics of mass marketing. Public relations people, with their emphasis on two-way communication, are in a good place to engage people in such conversations. This doesn't mean funneling all communication between an organization and its publics through a single person or office (or support page or voicemail system). To the contrary, a big part of the public relations function is to open an organization to direct conversations between people in the organization and people outside the organization who are interested in what the organization is doing. This markets-as-conversations approach echoes open-systems, peer-to-peer, two-way, and dialogic models of public relations.

It Depends

As discussed at the end of Chapter 1, Glen Cameron and his colleagues have worked to elaborate how the best approaches to successful public relations are not total advocacy or absolute accommodation (e.g., Cancel, Cameron, Sallot, & Mitrook, 1997; Reber & Cameron, 2003). In response to the idea that Grunig's symmetrical ideal of public relations might provide a single superior model for practice, they developed the contingency approach to describe how successful public relations means picking the point on the continuum that works best given the specifics of a situation.

Likewise, the best approach to online communications depends on the circumstances. Online media are perfectly capable of server-side, one-way, asymmetrical, denotative, monologic, and markets-as-targets approaches to public relations. There are times when it makes good sense to use them as such. But what makes online public relations exciting is closer to the other end of these continua, where the "real work of PR" is likely to occur (see Table 4.1). Online media are giving us new opportunities to practice more two-way, symmetrical, facilitative, dialogic, conversational public relations.

54 PUBLIC RELATIONS ONLINE

Table 4.1   Ranges of Choices for Online Media Use

Server-Side	Peer-to-Peer
One-way	Two-way
Asymmetrical	Symmetrical
Creator-type (denotative)	Facilitative
Monologic	Dialogic
Markets as targets	Markets as conversations

❖ NOTE

1. Van Ruler's (2004) concepts of denotative and connotative meaning are cited here in abbreviated form for their direct application to public relations practitioner typologies. She cites Littlejohn (1992) and Rosengren (2000) as sources of more general discussion of denotation and connotation in communication studies.

❖ REFERENCES

Arnett, R. (1981). Toward a phenomenological dialogue. *Western Journal of Speech Communication, 45,* 201–212.

Benkler, Y. (2006). *The wealth of networks: How social production transforms markets and freedom.* New Haven, CT: Yale Press.

BizRate shopping search. (2005). Retrieved June 9, 2006, from http://www .bizrate.com/ratings_guide/cust_reviews__mid—57946.html

Botan, C., & Taylor, M. (2004). Public relations: State of the field. *Journal of Communication, 54,* 645–661.

Buber, M. (1958). *I and thou* (2nd ed., R. G. Smith, Trans.). New York: Scribners.

Cancel, A. E., Cameron, G. T., Sallot, L. M., & Mitrook, M. A. (1997). It depends: A contingency theory of accommodation in public relations. *Journal of Public Relations Research, 9,* 31–63.

Case study—Hewlett-Packard (China)—IPG. (2004). Retrieved June 9, 2006, from http://www.bm.com/pages/cs/Hewlett

Coombs, W. T. (1998). The Internet as potential equalizer: New leverage in confronting social irresponsibility. *Public Relations Review, 24,* 289–303.

Heath, R. L. (1998). New communication technologies: An issues management point of view. *Public Relations Review, 24,* 273–288.

HIV at work case study. (2005). Retrieved June 9, 2006, from http://www .ogilvypr.com/case-studies/hiv-at-work.cfm

International community of women living with HIV/Aids. (2005). Retrieved June 9, 2006, from http://www.icw.org/tiki-view_articles.php

Internet. (n.d.). Retrieved June 9, 2006, from http://www.m-w.com/

Kent, M. L., & Taylor, M. (1998). Building dialogic relationships through the World Wide Web. *Public Relations Review, 24,* 321–334.

Leichty, G., & Springston, J. (1993). Reconsidering public relations models. *Public Relations Review, 19,* 327–339.

Littlejohn, S. W. (1992). *Theories of human communication* (5th ed.). Belmont, CA: Wadsworth.

Reber, B., & Cameron, G. T. (2003). Measuring contingencies: Using scales to measure public relations practitioner limits to accommodation. *Journalism and Mass Communication Quarterly, 80,* 431–446.

Rosengren, K. E. (2000). *Communication: An introduction.* London: Sage.

Searls, D., & Weinberger, D. (2001). Markets are conversations. In R. Levine, C. Locke, D. Searls, & D. Weinberger (Eds.), *The cluetrain manifesto: The end of business as usual* (pp. 75–114). New York: Perseus. Available from http://www.cluetrain.com/book/markets.html

van Ruler, B. (2004). The communication grid: An introduction of a model of four communication strategies. *Public Relations Review, 30,* 123–143.

Hands-Online Activity

❖ CASES IN POINT?

1. Search online for two separate public relations case studies in which online media were central to the strategy. Hint: Case studies are available through the Web sites of professional organizations such as the Public Relations Society of America (Silver Anvil Awards) and the Council of Public Relations Firms, and public relations agencies such as Ketchum and Ogilvy Worldwide.

2. Compare where the overall communication strategy (not the specific tactics) of each might fit on the continua in Table 4.1.

Case 1

Name of Case: _____
Briefly describe how online media were used:

Rate the overall communication strategy on a scale of 1 to 5 for each dimension:

Case 1: Overall Communication Strategy Was . . .				
Very one-way				Very two-way
1	2	3	4	5
Very asymmetrical				Very symmetrical
1	2	3	4	5
Very denotative (creator type)				Very facilitative
1	2	3	4	5
Very monologic				Very dialogic
1	2	3	4	5
Very markets-as-targets				Very markets-as-conversations
1	2	3	4	5

Case 2

Name of Case: _____
Briefly describe how online media were used:

Rate the overall communication strategy on a scale of 1 to 5 for each dimension:

Case 2: Overall Communication Strategy Was . . .				
Very one-way				Very two-way
1	2	3	4	5
Very asymmetrical				Very symmetrical
1	2	3	4	5
Very denotative (creator type)				Very facilitative
1	2	3	4	5
Very monologic				Very dialogic
1	2	3	4	5
Very markets-as-targets				Very markets-as-conversations
1	2	3	4	5

3. Was the one with the higher ratings better public relations than the other? Why or why not?

5

Relationships

❖ OVERVIEW

This chapter will look at the "relations" part of online public relations. Online media technologies, individual characteristics, and cultural characteristics of social groups are discussed as relational antecedents that must be in place before relationships are established online. Concepts borrowed from the field of interpersonal communication are then covered to help understand the underlying processes of online public relations. Finally, relational outcomes such as trust, commitment, satisfaction, and mutual control show the potential value of public relations in terms attuned to the experiences of real people using online media to communicate.

❖ FOCUSING ON RELATIONSHIPS

If we define public relations as a process of building and maintaining mutually beneficial relationships, then we ought to be able to say just what we mean by "relationships." Although no single definition is universally agreed on, here are a few solid working definitions of *relationship* in the context of public relations to get us started:

60   PUBLIC RELATIONS ONLINE

- "The state which exists between an organization and its key publics in which the actions of either entity impact the economic, social, political and/or cultural well-being of the other entity" (Ledingham & Bruning, 1998, p. 62).
- "Relationships consist of the transactions that involve the exchange of resources between organizations" (Broom, Casey, & Ritchey, 1997, p. 91).
- "Routinized, sustained patterns of behavior by individuals related to their involvement with an organization. . . . Many online relationships operate in tandem with offline relationships and thus are part of a total organizational-public relationship" (Hallahan, 2004, p. 775).

So how do we study relationships? This is an important question for academics, but it also is important for practitioners who want to be able to discuss the contributions of their work in ways more sophisticated than counting the number of names in a database or the number of hits on their Web pages. Although there are just about as many ways to study relationships as there are people taking on these studies, most seem to agree that the study of relationships can be broken down into antecedents, maintenance processes, and outcomes (Broom et al., 1997; Grunig & Huang, 2000; Hallahan, 2004; Hon & Grunig, 1999; Ledingham, 2003; Ledingham & Bruning, 1998). The remainder of this chapter will look at these three aspects of understanding the role of online media in public relations. This relational approach then can be used as a foundation for understanding how public relations people work with a wide variety of publics and organizations ranging from news media (Chapter 6), to consumers and investors (Chapter 7), to activists (Chapter 8).

❖ NOT-SO-SECRET INGREDIENTS FOR
     SUCCESS—RELATIONAL ANTECEDENTS

Relational antecedents are the things that need to be in line before relationships between organizations and publics can be established. We can look at three broad categories of antecedents for online relationships in public relations: (1) technologies, (2) the individuals who use the technologies, and (3) the social structures and cultures that give context to public-relations-type relationships.

Technologies. Kirk Hallahan (2003) of Colorado State University has identified several important factors that help determine how online computer systems can contribute to relationships. First is the actual computer gear. The range of online technologies, from server-side databases to broadband, multimedia group-conferencing systems, offers a broad spectrum of communication options for relationship building.

Media richness theory helps explain the important characteristics of this range. In the 1980s, organizational communication scientists Richard Daft and Robert Lengel (Daft & Lengel, 1984; Lengel, 1983) studied how media vary in their ability to carry information. They posited that each medium differs in (a) feedback capability, (b) number of cues used, (c) personal focus of source, and (d) language variety (Daft, Lengel, & Trevino, 1987). As shown in Table 5.1, studies rating various media illustrate a clear pattern in how media vary in richness (Irani & Kelleher, 1997). Placing newer media into the pattern isn't rocket science. A barebones, brochureware-type Web site would fall near the bottom of the list. Smooth-running videoconferencing technology would be richer than audio-only conferencing or standard telephone calls.

Media richness, then, is the potential of a particular medium to convey rich information. Media richness theorists suggest that richer media are better suited for handling more equivocal communication. *Equivocality* is the ambiguity, or lack of clarity, of information. Researchers consider information tasks that are very unambiguous with well-understood procedures to guide information-seeking behavior to be low in equivocality. Highly equivocal information tasks, on the other hand, leave room for "the existence of multiple and conflicting interpretations" (Daft et al., 1987, p. 357).

According to media richness theory, more equivocal information tasks—the kind that are likely to be involved in relationship management—call for richer media. Public relations people who report conducting more manager-level work (i.e., building and maintaining relationships) as opposed to technical tasks (i.e., disseminating information for others) also report using richer media more often (Kelleher, 2001).

Although face-to-face communication is still the gold standard, having access to richer media makes work easier for those trying to establish and maintain relationships online. Of course, both the public relations practitioner and the people she wants to communicate with must have access for these technologies to work. You might have an awesome video conferencing setup at your office, but it will not do you much good if the people you want to communicate with don't have access on the other end.

The concept of richness is just one way of understanding how characteristics of media technologies differ in ways that affect the

Table 5.1 Media Richness Ratings

	Lengel (1983)	*Trevino et al. (1988)*	*Daft et al. (1987)*	*Trevino et al. (1990)*	*D'Ambra & Rice (1994)*
Richest	Face-to-face	Face-to-face	Face-to-face	Face-to-face	Face-to-face
	Telephone	Telephone	Telephone	Telephone	Telephone
	Written personal (letters, memos)	E-mail	Written, addressed documents (note, memo, letter)	E-mail, letter	Voicemail, e-mail
	Written, formal (bulletins, documents)	Written		Note, memo	Business memo
Leanest	Numeric, formal (computer format)		Unaddressed documents (flier, bulletin, report)	Special report, flier/bulletin	

relationships among people using these technologies.[1] Yet any lasting concept describing media technologies in relationship management only matters to the degree that it affects how real people interact with those media.

Individual people. Before a relationship starts, individuals generally hold some prior knowledge about an organization or public and have attitudes about that group. If a person perceives an organization to be credible, he is more likely to enter into a relationship with that organization. When you are getting ready to make an online purchase from a company for the first time, how do you decide whether to give them your credit card number? Before you decide whether to delete or respond to an e-mail request, what do you take into consideration?

Relevant factors in an individual's decisions about whether or when to enter an online relationship include prior knowledge, attitudes, other communication activities, personalities, and goals (Hallahan, 2003). These are the factors you—as a public relations person—should consider before trying to initiate an online relationship with a reporter, a customer, or a vocal critic.

Put yourself in his or her shoes. Your assessment of an organization's credibility is based on what you already know about it, or others like it. Perhaps you already have a relationship with an organization offline, but you are considering moving that relationship online by making a purchase, answering an e-mail, or completing a survey. Your prior experiences with that organization are obviously going to affect your decisions.

How well individuals identify with an organization also comes into play. When I get a request to complete an online survey from a student at some distant university, I have a really hard time saying no, even if I have never met that student or anyone from her school. I wasn't always so amenable to surveys. After conducting a few surveys myself though, I now really identify with the researcher making a request. I'll even put up with some usability hassles (e.g., having to enter a password and scroll through multiple screens) that I would never tolerate from someone trying to sell me something. I often ask the researcher to send me the paper or article that results from the research. I'm more apt to start a relationship with this person because I can identify with him or her or the school. If the survey comes from a school where I attended or taught, I find it almost impossible not to answer.

Cultures. How social groups form and operate online also is an important factor in understanding how relationships get started. Consider how group blogs often come to define public or organizational cultures. Groups, instead of individuals, maintain many blogs, and these

64   PUBLIC RELATIONS ONLINE

groups often comprise people working in different places for different organizations. When this happens, the group blog defines the common interests of its contributors, thereby making the blog a defining feature of a new organization (or of a new public, depending on your perspective).

Slashdot.org is a prime example. Slashdot is so big, claiming to post millions of Web items for hundreds of thousands of readers, that many who visit the site might not even consider it a blog. Developed in 1997 by Rob Malda and Jeff Bates to provide "news for nerds" and "stuff that matters" (see http://slashdot.org), Slashdot's news, links, downloads, and commentary are open to editing and update by a number of Slashdot authors. Anyone logging on to Slashdot also can submit story ideas. Submissions are vetted by authors who select posts "with an eye towards whatever is going to make Slashdot be what it is for that particular day" (Slashdot FAQ [frequently asked questions], n.d.). The site focuses on news and resources for those working in or interested in the information technology industry, but topics extend beyond techni-cal articles to political and social commentaries and criticism.

But before firing off a press release with hopes of reaching those hundreds of thousands of readers, consider the following statement from Slashdot's FAQ (n.d.):

> Slashdot will certainly review press releases from anyone who chooses to submit them through our standard submission form. However, please be aware that your product/service/tradeshow might not be as interesting to us as it is to you, and we are rela-tively unlikely to select press releases to be posted to the Slashdot main page. You're welcome to try, but please use the form as our email boxes are already bursting at the seams with unwanted press releases that if printed, could easily wallpaper a large por-tion of the Pyramids at Giza.

Like most influential bloggers, the Slashdot authors take pride in the open-source nature of their work as a community. Understanding the meaning of "open-source" is a critical antecedent to relationship building with such a group. It drives their norms and expectations. It also illustrates how a group of individuals working together online in geographically dispersed teams produce communication coming from an organization or public group distinct from the individuals who make up that group.

Open-source software includes computer code that anyone can tinker with once they acquire it. A common explanation of such free software is that it is free as in "free speech," but not necessarily free as in "free beer" ("Free Software Definition," 2005). Open-source software is like a batch of cookies from a friend that comes with the recipe. You can make your own batch later, maybe changing some ingredients, to see if you can produce a snack more to your own taste. You might even share with friends the changes you made to see if they like your version of the recipe better than the original. Proprietary software, on the other hand, comes to you with protected coding that you will probably never see or alter. This is like buying cookies at the store that don't include a recipe. Homemade cookies are often better than store bought.

Slashdot and other grassroots media groups extend the open-source concept beyond software to their communication efforts in general. The basic idea, as Dan Gillmor (2004) puts it, is like online barn raising. As a technology columnist for the San Jose, California, *Mercury News*, Gillmor was intrigued with the idea that, collectively, his readers often knew more than he did about the topics he covered: "If my readers know more than I do (which I know they do), I can include them in the process of making my journalism better" (p. 18). This open-source concept demands a certain amount of transparency in communication. Off-the-record comments, privileged sources, and embargoed press releases make about as much sense in this context as secret ingredients on a recipe exchange site.

Words like *open-source, grassroots media*, and *transparency* define the expectations and norms of many of the Web's most influential online publics and organizations. Their culture is to make information available. The theory of *structuration* can help public relations people understand how online social structures can be seen as both the medium of communication as well as the outcome of communication efforts (Witmer, 2000). The way Slashdot.org has evolved is different than the way traditional news media have evolved. Both the blog-like technology and the open-source social spirit are the products of a reflexive process in which people make decisions on how to use the technology, which leads to different social patterns, which lead to new uses of the technology, and so on. So how do you get in?

Join the party.

Joining the party, so to speak, is easy enough for you as an individual. You can start by reading posts in an online community, getting a sense of the group's norms, and starting to participate when you feel comfortable. The only snag is that you will likely find the group's norms are not in line with standard practices in public relations (e.g., news releases on Slashdot.org). To have your organization communicate effectively with publics online, you might find that you need to start thinking of your organization as a public itself.

66   PUBLIC RELATIONS ONLINE

Microsoft was one of the first of major U.S. companies to take this approach by hosting its own employees' blogs on blogs.msdn.com. MSDN stands for Microsoft Developer's Network. Although Microsoft still makes proprietary software, the spirit of their communication seems to have made a move toward a more open-source approach. Microsoft bloggers still refer to "PR" as a separate function, though, suggesting that those who do public relations in an official capacity are not the ones doing most the communicating in this context. "On the positive side," according to Searls and Weinberger (2001):

By acknowledging that, inevitably, many people speak for a particular company in many different ways, the company can address one of the most important and difficult questions; How can a large company have conversations with hundreds of millions of people? (p. 110)

In all likelihood, groups like MSDN are good news for the development of relationships between organizations and their publics. In a study of people's perceptions of MSDN blogs, Barbara Miller and I found that the authentic individual-style communication commonly used in blogging (we called it the "conversational human voice") worked for MSDN bloggers in engendering relational outcomes such as trust, satisfaction, and commitment (Kelleher & Miller, 2006).

❖ BUILDING AND MAINTAINING
    RELATIONSHIPS—RELATIONAL PROCESSES

Once the antecedents of online relationships are in place, the process of building and maintaining those relationships can commence. At the individual level, Hallahan (2003) suggests that online relationships are built in a process that starts with awareness and then progresses along as individuals adopt relational knowledge, attitudes, and behaviors.

A major challenge for those taking the relational perspective in public relations, however, is figuring out how what we know about individuals in relationships can help us understand how organizations and publics get along in relationships. One lead we have that looks promising is the work of Laura Stafford and Dan Canary in the field of interpersonal communication. Stafford and Canary's (1991) taxonomy of *relational maintenance strategies* provides a theoretical link between strategies found to be effective in interpersonal communication and the group-based relational outcomes of interest in public relations.

Canary and Stafford's (1992) five maintenance strategies for interpersonal relationships include the following: positivity (interacting with partners in a cheerful, uncritical manner), openness (directly discussing the nature of the relationship and disclosing one's desires for the relationship), assurances (communicating one's desire to continue with the relationship), social networks (relying on common affiliations and relations), and sharing tasks (performing one's responsibilities).

These strategies may be applied to organizational relationships by shifting the focus of the communication strategies to public, rather than interpersonal relationships (Grunig & Huang, 2000; Hon & Grunig, 1999). For example, positivity and cooperation involve efforts an organization employs to make a relationship more enjoyable and productive for those involved, openness includes providing disclosure regarding the nature of the organization and information of value to audiences, assurances include communication that emphasizes the value of audience members, social networks involve an emphasis on common affiliations between organizations and publics, and sharing tasks may include asking for public involvement when appropriate.

I find it striking, but not accidental, that these same strategies also are accounted for in the literature on blogs, markets as conversations, grassroots media, and online public relations (see Table 5.2). These underlying themes are lasting concepts for changing media.

❖ EVALUATING RELATIONAL STRATEGIES—RELATIONSHIP OUTCOMES

In the mix of advertising, marketing, and other communication functions, public relations is unique in its ability to build and enhance relationships with a range of key publics via relational strategies. Organizational relationships, which may include professional, personal, or community relations, can increase organizational effectiveness; can reduce the cost of litigation, regulation, boycotts, and so forth; and may also contribute to an organization's financial well-being through shareholder, consumer, and donor support (Bruning & Ledingham, 1999).

Hon and Grunig (1999) developed the PR Relationship Measurement Scale to help practitioners assess their organization's longer-term relationships with key publics by focusing on the following four indicators of the quality of an organization-public relationship:

1. **Control mutuality** is the degree to which parties agree on issues of power and influence. This doesn't mean that everyone has to have

68   PUBLIC RELATIONS ONLINE

Table 5.2   Relational Maintenance Strategies

	Relational Maintenance Strategies— Interpersonal (e.g., Canary & Stafford, 1992)	Relational Maintenance Strategies— Public Relations (e.g., Grunig, Hon, Huang)	Markets as Conversations, Grassroots Media, Structuration (e.g., Searls & Weinberger, 2001; Gillmor, 2004; Witmer, 2000)
Positivity	"Interacting with the partner in a cheerful, optimistic and uncritical manner" (p. 243).	"Anything the organization or public does to make the relationship more enjoyable for the parties involved" (Hon & Grunig, 1999, p. 14).	"The Web is a funny place— literally. We learn a lot about the voices we hear through their humor" (Searls & Weinberger, 2001, p. 102).
Openness	"Directly discussing the nature of the relationship and disclosing one's desires for the relationship" (p. 243).	Disclosure	Transparency
Assurances	"Stress one's continuation in the relationship" (pp. 243–244).	"Attempts by parties in the relationship to assure the other parties that they and their concerns are legitimate" (Hon & Grunig 1999, p. 15).	Respect as a norm; legitimacy in structuration
Social networks	"Interacting with or relying on common affiliations and relatives" (p. 244).	"Organizations building networks with the same groups as their publics" (Grunig & Huang, 2000, p. 37).	Linked blogs, group blogs, grassroots media
Sharing tasks	"Performing one's responsibilities" (p. 244).	"Organizations' and publics' sharing in solving joint or separate problems" (Hon & Grunig, 1999, p. 14).	Open source

exactly equal power. People expect some imbalance, even in peer-to-peer relationships. But do you—or the group you belong to—have a say when it is appropriate? Online sales and auction sites allow users much more control in rating items and even setting prices than traditional modern marketplaces. This also applies to marketplaces of ideas such as Slashdot.

2. Trust includes dimensions of integrity, dependability, and competence. Before making an online purchase, do you trust that the organization is charging a fair price? This is integrity. Before registering your e-mail address with an online news service, do you trust that they will protect your privacy (and your inbox from spam)? This is dependability. Before making a donation to a nonprofit group, are you confident that they will be able to get your money where you believe it should go? This is competence.

3. Satisfaction is the degree to which parties feel favorably toward each other because positive expectations are met. This is what organizations are trying to determine when they ask you to rate how helpful the contents of their help pages were.

4. Commitment is the degree to which parties believe that the relationship is worthwhile to continue. Will you renew your subscription to that e-newsletter? Will you update your contact information with your alma mater's alumni office when you get a new e-mail account?

Most of these examples are indicators regarding the quality of what public relations scholars call *exchange relationships*. In an exchange relationship, parties are willing to provide benefits because comparable benefits are expected in return. This is the foundation of basic marketing theory: I'll pay the price if you deliver the product. In the most basic exchange relationships, when the customer's goal (relational antecedent) is simply to make a one-time purchase, terms like *dialogue* and *structuration* are practically irrelevant (Len-Rios, 2001). Exchange relationships also apply in employee relations: I'll do the work if you write the paycheck. But relationships based *only* on the promise of a paycheck are as hollow as the halfhearted *"mayIhelpyou"* you get from an unengaged "customer service representative" working the business end of an 800-number help line. In South Korea, for example, better organizational climates have been shown to be the result of communication factors more consistent with communities than marketing models (Jo & Shim, 2005).

In a *communal relationship,* both parties provide benefits without expecting any immediate return. Rather, they provide benefits out of

70   PUBLIC RELATIONS ONLINE

concern for the welfare of the other. This may sound touchy-feely at first, but communal relationships matter in terms of job satisfaction, customer loyalty, and the self-forming online markets that are driving newer models of e-commerce (Searls, 2004). As Hon and Grunig (1999) put it, "The role of public relations is to convince management that it also needs communal relationships with publics such as employees, the community, government, media, and stockholders" (p. 21). Not only do communal relationships help organizations attain positive outcomes, but they also help deter negative outcomes such as lawsuits, worker strikes, boycotts, and smear campaigns.

Finally, we should keep in mind the subtle but important distinction between one-to-one, one-to-many, and many-to-many communication. Even relationships between organizations and publics (both are *groups* of people) involve communication between *individuals* as members of those groups. Although the public relations outcomes often are seen as relationships among groups, the communication that leads to these relationships involves real, individual people—survey respondents, critics, consumers, journalists, constituents, donors, employees, members, and so forth.

❖ NOTE

1. The concepts of *usability* (Nielsen, 2000), *attributes of innovations* (Rogers, 2003), and *social presence* (Walther, 1992) are also worth exploring.

❖ REFERENCES

Broom, G. M., Casey, S., & Ritchey, J. (1997). Toward a concept and theory of organization-public relationships. *Journal of Public Relations Research, 9,* 83–98.

Bruning, S. D., & Ledingham, J. A. (1999). Relationships between organizations and publics: development of a multi-dimension organization-public relationship scale. *Public Relations Review, 25,* 157–158.

Canary, D. J., & Stafford, L. (1992). Relational maintenance strategies and equity in marriage. *Communication Monographs, 59,* 243–267.

Daft, R. L., & Lengel, R. H. (1984). Information richness: A new approach to managerial information processing and organizational design. In L. L. Cummings & B. M. Staw (Eds.), *Research in organizational behavior* (pp. 191–233). Greenwich, CT: JAI Press.

Daft, R. L., Lengel, R. H., & Trevino, L. K. (1987). Message equivocality, media selection, and manager performance: Implications for information systems. *MIS Quarterly, 11,* 355–366.

D'Ambra, J., & Rice, R. E. (1994). Multimethod approaches for the study of computer-mediated communication, equivocality and media selection. *IEEE Transactions on Professional Communication, 37*, 231–239.

Free Software Definition. (2005). Retrieved June 12, 2006, from http://www.gnu.org/philosophy/free-sw.html

Gillmor, D. (2004). *We the media: Grassroots journalism by the people, for the people*. Sebastopol, CA: O'Reilly.

Grunig, J. E., & Huang, Y. (2000). From organization effectiveness to relationship indicators: Antecedents of relationships, public relations strategies, and relationship outcomes. In J. A. Ledingham & S. D. Bruning (Eds.), *Public relations as relationship management: A relational approach to the study and practice of public relations* (pp. 23–53). Hillsdale, NJ: Lawrence Erlbaum Associates.

Hallahan, K. (2003, May). *A model for assessing Web sites as tools in building organizational-public relationships*. Paper presented to the public relations division at the annual convention of the International Communication Association, San Diego, CA.

Hallahan, K. (2004). Online public relations. In H. Bidgoli (Ed.), *The Internet encyclopedia* (Vol. 2, pp. 769–783). Hoboken, NJ: John Wiley.

Hon, L. C., & Grunig, J. E. (1999). *Guidelines for measuring relationships in public relations*. Gainesville, FL: Institute for Public Relations. Retrieved June 12, 2006, from http://www.instituteforpr.com/pdf/1999_guide_measure_relationships.pdf

Irani, T., & Kelleher, T. (1997, August). *Information task equivocality and media richness: Implications for health information on the World Wide Web*. Paper presented to the communication theory and methodology division at the annual convention of the Association for Education in Journalism and Mass Communication, Chicago.

Jo, S., & Shim, S. W. (2005). Paradigm shift of employee communication: The effect of management communication on trusting relationships. *Public Relations Review, 31*, 277–280.

Kelleher, T. (2001). Public relations roles and media choice. *Journal of Public Relations, Research, 13*, 303–320.

Kelleher, T., & Miller, B. M. (2006). Organizational blogs and the human voice: Relational strategies and relational outcomes. *Journal of Computer-Mediated Communication, 11*(2), Article 1. Retrieved June 12, 2006, from http://jcmc.indiana.edu/vol11/issue2/kelleher.html

Ledingham, J. A. (2003). Explicating relationship management as a general theory of public relations. *Journal of Public Relations Research, 15*, 181–198.

Ledingham, J. A. & Bruning, S. D. (1998). Relationship management in public relations: Dimensions of an organization-public relationship. *Public Relations Review, 24*, 55–65.

Lengel, R. H. (1983). *Managerial information processing and communication-media source selection behavior*. Unpublished PhD dissertation, Texas A & M University.

Len-Rios, M. E. (2001). *Playing by the rules: Relationships with online users.* Gainesville, FL: Institute for Public Relations. Retrieved June 12, 2006, from http://www.instituteforpr.com/ winning_papers.phtml? article_id= 2001_playing_rules

Nielsen, J. (2000). *Designing usability.* Indianapolis: IN: New Rider.

Rogers, E. M. (2003). *Diffusion of innovations* (5th ed.). New York: Free Press.

Searls, D. (2004, September 7). *The independence revolution: How self-forming markets are changing business, technology, and everything else.* Retrieved June 12, 2006, from http://www.ibiblio.org/speakers/searls/

Searls, D., & Weinberger, D. (2001). Markets are conversations. In R. Levine, C. Locke, D. Searls, & D. Weinberger (Eds.), *The cluetrain manifesto: The end of business as usual* (pp. 75–114). New York: Perseus.

Slashdot FAQ. (n.d.). Retrieved June 12, 2006, from http://slashdot.org/faq/

Stafford, D. J., & Canary, L. (1991). Maintenance strategies and romantic relationship type, gender and relational characteristics. *Journal of Social and Personal Relationships, 8,* 217–242.

Trevino, L. K., Daft, R. L., & Lengel, R. H. (1990). Understanding managers' media choices: A symbolic interactionist perspective. In J. Fulk & C. W. Steinfield (Eds.), *Organizations and communication technology.* Newbury Park, CA: Sage.

Trevino, L. K., Lengel, R. H., Bodensteiner, W., & Gerloff, E. (1988, August). *Managerial media choice: The interactive influences of cognitive style and message equivocality.* Paper presented at the meeting of the Academy of Management, Anaheim, CA.

Walther, J. B. (1992). Interpersonal effects in computer-mediated interaction: A relational perspective. *Communication Research, 19,* 52–90.

Witmer, D. F. (2000). *Spinning the web: A handbook for public relations on the Internet.* New York: Longman.

Hands-Online Activity

❖ LURK AND LEARN

Lurk among an active online public or organization. In other words, find a discussion board, chatroom, blog page, or other Web site where people actively are engaged in posting daily communications on businesses or topics of interest to them. Then browse around silently just to observe what's going on. Here are some examples of top-level sites that lead to more specific forums. Lurk in one of these, or find another forum closer to your own interests:

- http://slashdot.org/
- http://chat.yahoo.com/ (Yahoo registration required)
- http://www.news-record.com/news/local/blogs.html
- http://www.crookedtimber.org/

1. What are the group's norms and expectations that would be most important to understand before trying to establish a relationship with other users?

2. Write three rules you would you make for yourself before contributing to the group.

3. Could you do public relations there? How?

6

News-Driven Relationships

❖ OVERVIEW

To many people, public relations is publicity, and they're right . . . sort of. Publicity is undeniably a very large part of public relations work—a point that will be underscored in this chapter. Public relations people must consider both push and pull strategies in engaging journalists and others in interactive, news-driven relationships. To be effective in online news operations, public relations practitioners design and manage online communications with journalistic values in mind.

❖ PUBLICITY IN THE BIG PICTURE

The whole idea of publicity—getting news out—is sometimes seen as the primary task of public relations. Let's say a public relations practitioner e-mails a news release to a reporter who takes some of that word-processed information and pastes it into a news story, which is then published in a large-circulation traditional newspaper. If the public relations person sees his job as done at that point—if he sees publicity as an

76   PUBLIC RELATIONS ONLINE

end in itself—that's server-side public relations. That's the town crier or the publicist at the top of his game. Yet even a publicity-focused promoter needs to build and maintain relationships with news media to be effective in the long run. Interactive communication is still critical.

When media relations are going well, public relations people provide journalists with useful and accurate information, and journalists report fairly and accurately on topics of interest to the public relations people and the organizations they represent. Over time, sources and reporters may develop mutually dependent relationships in which public relations people speak for their organizations and journalists report news in the public interest. Such symbiotic source-reporter relationships are easily seen as interactive relationships at the interpersonal level, regardless of whether the publicity generated serves organizations and publics as a tool for one-way communication or as an open line in an open conversation. These relationships are interactive because what journalists report often depends on what public relations people provide, and in turn, public relations people often act and communicate based on what they learn from journalists.

In any case, online media can ease the communication between public relations people and journalists as well as other news-driven publics such as bloggers.

❖ ONLINE MEDIA RELATIONS—WHAT
    NEEDS TO BE IN PLACE?

The antecedents of news-driven relationships include factors related to the technology of online communications, the people themselves, and the cultures in which people work (Hallahan, 2003).

Technology and Content

Web sites. Web sites designed for news media are often labeled pressrooms, newsrooms, media centers, or news centers. In 2001, Coy Callison of Texas Tech University analyzed a sample of 195 Fortune 500 sites with pressroom-type Web pages (Callison, 2003). Table 6.1 shows the elements Callison (2003) found most common (those included in at least 10% of the sites). These features are listed side-by-side with recommendations made by Kent and Taylor (2003) and O'Keefe (2002) to give you a sense of what a typical pressroom might contain. Online vendors provide help with these tools and tactics (for a fee, of course). The standard services offered by such vendors may help explain the consistencies in Table 6.1.

Table 6.1   Typical Contents of Online Pressrooms

Callison's (2003) Most Common in Fortune 500 Pressrooms	Kent and Taylor's (2003) Checklist for Media Relevance	O'Keefe's (2002) "What should the site contain?"
Press releases or news releases (97%)	News releases	Current news
Contact information (75%)	Contact information for public	Contact information
Executive bios or profiles (51%)	Bios of key organizational members	Staff profiles
Executive photographs (49%)	High-quality, downloadable graphics	Artwork
Company fact sheets (35%)	Fact sheets	Product and service descriptions
Annual reports— financial (34%)	Annual reports	Financial information
Company history (32%)	History of organization	Corporate history
News alert service for media (31%)		Opt-in news service
Company staff speeches or presentations (30%)	Downloadable speeches or commercials	Speeches and other transcripts
Product or company in-action photos (28%)	High-quality, downloadable graphics	Product and service descriptions
Press release search engine (26%)	Searchable archive	News release archive
Company logos for use in publication (23%)	High-quality, downloadable graphics	Artwork
Media kits (21%)	E-media kits (backgrounders)	Press kits
Corporate profile (20%)		
Quarterly reports— financial (17%)		Financial information
Material presented in archived video (17%)		Multimedia archives
Company philanthropic activity (16%)		Community activities
News published and aired about company (16%)	Links to stories about your organization	
Company perspective pieces on issues and trends (10%)	Position papers	Legislative initiatives

78   PUBLIC RELATIONS ONLINE

Press releases and news releases. As text author and senior public relations counselor Fraser Seitel (2001) put it, press releases are "the granddaddy of public relations writing vehicles" (p. 255). Given that your news-driven publics include bona fide journalists as well as others who read and report news online, the term *news release* seems to work better online than *press release*.

Keep in mind too that many online news services provide information almost directly from the sources, blurring the line between news releases and news stories. For example, Science*Daily* (www .sciencedaily.com) reprints news release text from sources such as NASA, universities, and professional associations that report scientific advances. Science*Daily* includes links at the bottom of such stories to the original source.

Online news releases can be useful to disseminate information to already-interested audiences. Those who work in science communication at NASA sometimes call the people who read their stories and visit sites like Science*Daily* "science interested." But if you are relying on journalists to take your news beyond your actively topic-interested publics, you will probably want to extend your communications well beyond the effort it takes to simply post a news release on a Web site.

News releases can be distributed to journalists through paid wire services such as Business Wire (http://www.businesswire.com/), PR Newswire (http://www.prnewswire.com/), or Bacon's Information (http://www.bacons.com/). Distribution services allow you to feed your news to targeted media contacts in local, regional, national, or global news organizations.

Questionable Claims

❖ USING ONLINE MEDIA TO CUT OUT THE MIDDLEMAN

On the sliding scale that goes from controlled to uncontrolled communication tactics, sending a press release to a journalist weighs heavily at the uncontrolled end.

So why bother—especially online where you can post your own news as easily as you can "release" it to the press? The most common answers are cost and credibility. Placing a news release doesn't carry the direct costs you have to pay to place advertising. If you pay for an ad, part of what you get for your money is some control of when, where, and how that ad will be presented. Of course, you'll find costs in placing news releases too (e.g., employee salaries, fees for media distribution services, the costs of charitable donations or special events that make your organization newsworthy in the first place), but publicity is generally thought of as cheaper than advertising.

And what about credibility? Common wisdom holds that if a journalist covers your story, publics will see that information as much more credible than if you deliver the news directly. Having a third party deliver a message gives it more credibility . . . . Or does it?

Research calling this assumption into question has yielded mixed results. Hallahan (1999), for example, looked at the findings of 11 different experiments, and found "only qualified support" for the claim that publicity is superior to advertising in terms of credibility. He attributed much of the advantage of publicity over advertising to people's predispositions about news as opposed to their predispositions about advertising.

In a more recent analysis, Callison and Youngblood (2004) concluded that research has "established that the public does in fact attribute bias to practitioners and their messages that speak favorably of employers, which ultimately negatively affects the credibility of both" (p. 8). They then ran an experiment and found that undergraduate students who read information attributed to news media rated it as more credible than students who read the same information when it was attributed to a corporate source. As for media differences, information presented on corporate Web sites was seen as less credible than the same information delivered in basic paper formats. In this case, the research supports common wisdom. The upshot is that just because online technologies make it easy to do so, online corporate communicators shouldn't be too quick to "cut out the middleman," as Callison and Youngblood put it.

Other sources. On the other side of the news cycle, "reporters" of all levels, from a United Press International bureau chief to a high school MySpace blogger, now can get their news from a number of competing sources with much greater speed than the days before the rise of online media. Consider this advice for aspiring online journalists from *Online Journalism Review* at the University of Southern California, Annenberg School of Journalism: "Online reporters can find thousands of stories lurking within public data. Government databases on crime, school test scores, population statistics, accident reports, environmental safety and more can keep a motivated writer busy for years" ("How to Report a News Story Online," n.d.).

Trends in how this information is communicated tell us something about how online media are changing the way people manage publicity efforts in a competitive information environment. For example, iPressroom, a Los Angeles-based vendor, reported that between

80   PUBLIC RELATIONS ONLINE

November 2005 and February 2006, the number of inquiries for press-room tools and services (mostly pull media) exceeded requests for news wire distribution (push media) for the first time in the organization's history. "And beyond just making sure people can find your news on the Web, the real opportunity of online PR is using your news to introduce constituents to your online presence, by participating in relevant digital conversations," said Eric Schwartzman, the company's president ("Internet Pressrooms Displace News Distribution," 2006).

> Much as the news of the day presents an opportunity to get a company, brand or product in front of the media, that same information online presents an opportunity to attract and build a digital constituency, by providing people with information when they want it, rather than when you decide to push it over the news wire. ("Internet Pressrooms," 2006)

In fact, the "news cycle" as we once knew it has changed dramatically. Daily newspapers and nightly news broadcasts no longer set the pace for the interactive exchange between sources and reporters. Making information available immediately regardless of the time of day is now much more important. The characteristics of online media ease the process of keeping up with a perpetual news cycle that might revolve in minutes rather than hours or days.

Alerts, feeds, and RSS. Timeliness, of course, is a major news value. One way to address the issue of whether the news you post online is seen as actual news, as opposed to "archives," is to let key publics know the minute you post it. As you establish relationships with news-driven publics online and off, you might ask them if you can include them on an e-mail list for news alerts—what O'Keefe (2002) calls an opt-in news service. Account executives at Edelman, working for Wal-Mart, have extended the opt-in idea to bloggers by getting in touch with key bloggers to see if they're interested, then "feeding them exclusive nuggets of news, suggesting topics for postings and even inviting them to visit its corporate headquarters" (Barbaro, 2006).

RSS and related syndication and subscription technologies such as podcasting come into play by helping public relations people balance their interest in getting information out with journalists' and others' interest in filtering for relevant information. Retaining the plus sides of Web pages and e-mail, RSS allows you to publish information at any time. But RSS also gives control to subscribers to only receive feeds from people and organizations from whom they want to hear. You might set up a newsroom RSS feed that only includes information that certain news-driven publics would find interesting. Reporters, bloggers, and anyone else who subscribes can then check their feeds separately from their e-mail to get summaries of new posts from your organization. These feeds can include news-release material as well as basic announcements of special events, interview opportunities, or changes in contact information.

By including recent RSS posts blog-style (reverse chronological with links, etc.) in your online pressroom, you allow people to see a sample of the type of information they would get immediately if they subscribed to the feed. So, if a journalist covering your company visits your pressroom on June 22 and learns from an archived news release that a new vice president was hired on June 1, she might just blow that off as old news. But if she sees that the story had been posted immediately as an RSS feed and that she could have had that story delivered to her own news aggregator on June 1 (or maybe even earlier), she might see the benefit in subscribing for future news tips. RSS subscriptions can be password verified, but consider carefully whether controlling access is a good idea from the perspective of those you hope will subscribe.

Newsworthy content—the good, bad, and ugly. As shown in Table 6.1, many organizations include philanthropic efforts in their online pressrooms, but considering the perspectives of news-driven publics means questioning how newsworthy such information is. Although it is common practice to tell people about all the good things your organization is doing, especially when those things are newsworthy based on their currency and positive effect, remember that struggle, conflict, and negative effects also are news values. If your Web site, RSS feeds, and the like are blatantly blind to any bad news, your online communications will be of far less news value to serious journalists. Just ignoring the bad and the ugly news probably is not the best way to convince people that you're really concerned about helping them report. And online, if you don't comment, someone else will.

During a conflict or crisis, people, especially journalists and bloggers, are going to report about your organization anyway, so you might as well work with them to make sure your side of the story gets out quickly and accurately.

As a final piece of advice for setting up online news operations, remember to make information that is treated legally and ethically as public information easily available. Again, there's no use hiding information—good or bad—that a reporter can and should access while covering your organization. Links to certain financial reports, legislative actions, and published position papers ought to be easily accessible.

82   PUBLIC RELATIONS ONLINE

The spirit of openness and transparency, of course, is as much about human attitudes and relational processes as it is about technology.

Journalists as People—Pushing, Pulling, Tugging, Dancing

The concepts of push and pull media show how understanding the role of technology in public relations means understanding how actual people use the technologies of online communication. Although we must consider bloggers, investors, consumers, donors, federal regulators, and a host of other digital constituents in news operations, the relationships between professional public relations people and professional journalists illustrate the balance between organizational interests and public interests particularly well. The pros, after all, have been at this a long time and have developed norms and procedures for professional practice that apply across media platforms.

When public relations people push an appropriate amount of information, and when journalists feel they can pull the information they need, a dance metaphor fits the source-reporter information exchange. When journalists get frustrated by the amount or quality of information coming from public relations people, or when public relations people irritate journalists by over-jockeying to manage the news, the battle for control is better described as a tug of war. Whereas public relations people value advocacy, journalists value independent balance. As stated in the Society of Professional Journalists' (1996) code of ethics, it is their job to "distinguish between advocacy and news reporting" and to "deny favored treatment to advertisers and special interests and resist their pressure to influence news coverage."

But public relations people do have influence in the news process, and this influence does not necessarily lead to unethical favored treatment. Public relations scholars call this influence "information subsidies," meaning that public relations professionals support the work of journalists by giving them pieces of information that they value (Shin & Cameron, 2003, p. 253). Online media offer us many formats for delivering information, but the value of that information depends on the values of the journalists who receive it.

Dancing well online requires a keen respect for journalists' interest in fairness, independence, timeliness, and accuracy:

- **Respect journalists' independence and fairness** by getting your side of the story out while realizing that journalists are also inclined, if not obligated, to get other sides of the story. You might even help them find these other sources online if you can. If your nonprofit group is

News-Driven Relationships   83

involved in a community issue, consider participating in an open Web forum on that issue and inviting journalists to the discussion.

• **Respect deadlines and deadline pressure.** Keep your Web site current. Send short e-mails. Keep Web content concise. Use links in e-mails and Web pages to give journalists access to more detailed information while keeping the "pitch" short. Schedule Webcasts at times that will allow journalists to meet editorial deadlines.

• **Respect accuracy.** Check your general facts—this is easier online than it has ever been before. With online access, you've got a world-class almanac, dictionary, encyclopedia, atlas, and entire library at your fingertips (Goldsborough, 2002). And for goodness sake, edit for grammar and fact errors. Sure, online writing is usually more casual than offline printing, but fact errors and sloppy grammar will still fly red flags indicating questionable professional credibility. Of course, you are expected to be the authority on the organization you represent. If you post or e-mail a mistake that gets published by a journalist and the embarrassing error ends up under her byline, no doubt you will have damaged the relationship.

Culture in Media Relations

National and geographical diversity. We must consider how international and cultural norms affect the source-reporter relationship online, where we may cross national and geographical boundaries every time we log on. Unlike picking up the phone and making a call to a friend who works at the local TV news station, effective online media relations demands that you extend your perspective beyond your local cultural and professional norms and values.

Just as you might do research on a foreign country before traveling there, you ought to try to get an understanding of regional differences in source-reporter role expectations before extending your online media relations efforts beyond your own cyber-backyard.

For example, U.S. practitioners might find Asian news media in countries such as India, Korea, and Japan to be even more untrusting of official organizational communications than journalists in the United States. Journalists in these countries are likely to favor less-direct forms of communication such as dinners, social outings, and cocktail parties (Sriramesh, Kim, & Takasaki, 1999). Sriramesh et al. (1999) calls this the personal influence model of public relations. Van Ruler (2004) might call it the steward model as it applies in Europe. But how might such differences play out online?

84   PUBLIC RELATIONS ONLINE

According to international public relations scholars Jae-Hwa Shin and Glen Cameron (2003), "Technological change passes through the filter of the cultural context, being altered in subtle ways by cultural mores and news-gathering practices" (p. 255). Exploring the idea that Korean professionals are more likely to prefer offline social interactions, they looked at how South Korean and U.S. journalists and public relations practitioners perceived the following online source-reporter contacts: e-mail news releases, multimedia press kits, streaming clips, Web chatting, homepages, Web site pressrooms, Internet conferences, and online discussions. They found that journalists and public relations people in Korea are in closer agreement on the influence and credibility of offline contact such as phone calls, speeches, private meetings, and even golf outings than journalists and public relations people in the United States. Shin and Cameron suggested that Korean public relations professionals and journalists place a greater value on face-to-face "human factors" in source-reporter relationships than media professionals in the United States.

This is not to say that South Korean media professionals are pessimistic about the use of online technology, but it does show how U.S. public relations practitioners place different values on online contact than Korean journalists and even U.S. journalists. Shin and Cameron (2003) advise public relations people in both cultures to improve the outcomes of online international source-reporter relationships by providing resourceful, timely, accurate, and easily obtained news.

Pat Curtin and Kenn Gaither (2004) analyzed 10 English-language government Web sites in the Middle East and found that, by Western standards, online media relations (e.g., press releases) are not integral to the online international public information functions of these governments. Rather, they described what they found as "executive showcasing" more in line with Sriramesh's personal influence model, concluding that "who says something is more important than what is said" in many instances of online governmental public relations in the Middle East (Curtin & Gaither, 2004, p. 33, citing Zaharna, 1995). But this notion is not entirely foreign to Western public relations, particularly in sports and entertainment communications. Organizational culture and journalistic beats also have an influence in online source-reporter relationships.

Organizational and beat diversity. A U.S.-based computer-magazine writer will differ from an Australian sports broadcaster, who will differ from a Tanzanian government reporter in how he feels about public relations people as online sources of information. In addition to national and geographical differences, the news-gathering routines of different news organizations and different beats will come into play.

Hachigian and Hallahan (2003) surveyed computer-industry journalists in the United States to see how they perceived public relations Web sites. They found that computer-industry journalists' preferences for online public relations material were positively related to three things: their overall use of online media, their perceptions of the content value of online information, and the reputation of the source. The last item—source reputation—seems right in line with Sriramesh et al.'s (1999) personal influence model, showing some commonality among news routines across cultural and international boundaries.

In broad-sampled surveys and content analyses, public relations practitioners working in science communication, corporate communications, and university relations all have been found to make regular use of the Web in their efforts to establish visibility, credibility, and support. But the results show that online public relations efforts are often weak, failing to take full advantage of the Web's ability to deliver comprehensive content, useful links, and strategically valuable data for evaluating media relations outcomes (Connolly-Ahern & Broadway, 2004; Duke, 2002; Silverman, 2004).

❖ MAKING YOURSELF USEFUL

News media are working themselves into a frenzy about shark attacks as I write today. In the past week, one shark killed a swimmer and another seriously injured a fisherman, both in a small area of coastline in the Florida Panhandle. The story has grown from simple reporting on the details of the attacks to full-length features on sharks and shark encounters. If you were a journalist asked to produce a magazine piece or an extended feature segment on shark attacks, wouldn't you be interested in the following?

- Your readers' or viewers' risk of being bitten by an animal in New York City or injured in an accident involving home-improvement equipment relative to the risk of being attacked by a shark
- Comprehensive shark-attack data (1990 to date) and long-term trends in the past century, including data by nation, state, and even county
- Statistics on the Florida population and tourism trends as related to shark attack incidents

86   PUBLIC RELATIONS ONLINE

These are just a small sample of the data that researchers (and public relations people, no doubt) at the Florida Museum of Natural History have made available on their Web site for the "International Shark Attack File" (http://www.flmnh.ufl.edu/fish/Sharks/ISAF/ISAF.htm). Do you see how they have made themselves useful as resources in the journalistic task of storytelling?

A Google news search, limited to only articles occurring in recognized news media in the past 30 days, for the exact phrase *Florida Museum of Natural History* returned 1,180 results. No wonder the very first result returned for a basic Google search on the two words *shark attack* is a link to the Florida Museum of Natural History.

At the level of online publicity, there may be no greater reward than seeing your organization's Web page as the top result returned on a Google search. But as John Guiniven (2005) at Elon University put it in his "Ask the Professor" column in *Public Relations Tactics*, trends such as the rise of blogs, open-source movements, and nontraditional reporting mean that online public relations is about much more than online publicity through traditional journalistic channels. Strategic online public relations, he predicts, will more often take place in "an uncontrolled, two-way environment" (p. 6). Concepts like peer-to-peer networking, push/pull media, and contingency interactivity remind us that even publicity is about real relationships with real people.

❖ REFERENCES

Barbaro, M. (2006, March 7). Wal-Mart enlists bloggers in P.R. campaign. *New York Times*. Retrieved June 13, 2006, from http://www.nytimes.com/2006/03/07/technology/07blog.html?ei=5070&en=755590375e1d73ca&ex=1144987200

Callison, C. (2003). Media relations and the Internet: How Fortune 500 Company Web sites assist journalists in news gathering. *Public Relations Review, 29,* 29–41.

Callison, C., & Youngblood, N. E. (2004, August). *Cutting out the middle man: Must public relations messages be filtered through traditional news media to gain credibility?* Paper presented to the public relations division at the annual convention of the Association for Education in Journalism and Mass Communication, Toronto, Canada.

Connolly-Ahern, C., & Broadway, S. C. (2004, August). *The importance of appearing competent: An analysis of corporate impression management strategies on the World Wide Web.* Paper presented to the public relations division at the annual convention of the Association for Education in Journalism and Mass Communication, Toronto, Canada.

Curtin, P., & Gaither, T. K. (2004). International agenda-building in cyberspace: A study of Middle East government English-language Web sites. *Public Relations Review, 30*, 25–36.

Duke, S. (2002). Wired science: Use of the World Wide Web and e-mail in science and public relations. *Public Relations Review, 28*, 311–324.

Goldsborough, R. (2002, November). Getting your facts straight with a little help from the Web. *Public Relations Tactics, 9*(11), 6.

Guiniven, J. (2005, June). Examining the continuing influence of the Internet. *Public Relations Tactics, 12*(6), 6.

Hachigian, D., & Hallahan, K. (2003). Perceptions of public relations Web sites by computer industry journalists. *Public Relations Review, 29*, 43–62.

Hallahan, K. (1999). No, Virginia, it's not true what they say about publicity's "implied third-party endorsement" effect. *Public Relations Review, 25*, 331–350.

Hallahan, K. (2003, May). *A model for assessing Web sites as tools in building organizational-public relationships.* Paper presented to the public relations division at the annual convention of the International Communication Association, San Diego, CA.

How to report a news story online. (n.d.) *Online Journalism Review.* Retrieved June 13, 2006, from http://www.ojr.org/ojr/wiki/Reporting/

Internet pressrooms displace news distribution as most in-demand by public relations industry. (2006, March 19). *New Media Marketing Newsletter.* Retrieved June 13, 2006, from http://ipressroom.com/pr/corporate/info/Online-Influencer-Newsletter-Mar-2006.asp#1

Kent, M. L., & Taylor, M. (2003). Maximizing media relations: A Web site checklist. *Public Relations Quarterly, 48*(1), 14–18.

O'Keefe, S. (2002). *Complete guide to Internet publicity: Creating and launching successful online campaigns.* New York: John Wiley & Sons.

Seitel, F. P. (2001). *The practice of public relations* (8th ed.). Upper Saddle River, NJ: Prentice Hall.

Shin, J., & Cameron, G. T. (2003). The interplay of professional and cultural factors in the online source-reporter relationship. *Journalism Studies, 4*, 253–272.

Silverman, D. A. (2004, August). *Reaching key publics online: University public relations practitioners' use of the World Wide Web.* Paper presented to the public relations division at the annual convention of the Association for Education in Journalism and Mass Communication, Toronto, Canada.

Society of Professional Journalists. (1996). *SPJ Code of ethics.* Indianapolis, IN: Author. Retrieved June 13, 2006, from http://www.spj.org/ethics.asp

Sriramesh, K., Kim, Y., & Takasaki, M. (1999). Public relations in three Asian cultures: An analysis. *Journal of Public Relations Research, 11*, 271–292.

van Ruler, B. (2004). The communication grid: An introduction of a model of four communication strategies. *Public Relations Review, 30*, 123–143.

Zaharna, R. S. (1995). Understanding cultural preferences of Arab communication patterns. *Public Relations Review, 21*, 241–255.

88   PUBLIC RELATIONS ONLINE

Hands-Online Activity

❖ NEWSWORTHINESS ONLINE

Surf Business Wire (http://www.businesswire.com/) or PR Newswire
(http://www.prnewswire.com/). Take the perspective of a journalist.

1. List the headlines, dates, and times for the five most recently
    posted stories.

    a.
    b.
    c.
    d.
    e.

2. Rank the stories in order from 1 = *most likely to get published* to
    5 = *most likely to get trashed*.

3. What makes your Number 1 ranking newsworthy?

4. Go back online a few days later and use unique key words from
    the releases to search for any stories that were "placed" from
    your list. If you find any, how were they used? Were you able
    to predict which ones would get published?

7

Commerce-Driven Relationships

There is a generation growing up not used to reading newspapers and that is looking for less mediated engagement, and they're not particularly interested in looking for a press release translated by a writer and interpreted by an editor.

—*Wired* Magazine editor-in-chief Chris Anderson, in a speech delivered to Silicon Valley Public Relations Society of America members (as cited in O'Brien, 2005)

❖ OVERVIEW

As more and more commerce moves online, public relations departments face challenges in determining their role when it comes to generating and maintaining online business. This chapter will discuss how online technologies, individual people, and cultures all come into play in building and maintaining dollar- (or yen-, or euro-, or franc- . . .) driven relationships. Effective employee relations, customer relations, investor

90   PUBLIC RELATIONS ONLINE

relations, and donor relations mean taking the perspective of the employees, customers, investors, and donors with whom you have conversations online.

❖ WHAT NEEDS TO BE IN PLACE?

In a world of employee intranets, e-commerce, online investor relations, and Internet-based fundraising, the antecedents of online relationships are still about the technologies people use, the people themselves, and the diversity of cultures in which they live, work, and play—and buy, sell, and trade.

Technology and Content

Whereas P2P stands for "peer to peer" in computer networking, B2B is short for "business to business," and B2C is short for "business to consumer." Each refers to a basic relationship to identify a category of technologies. B2B applications often are designed to save humans time by automating tedious tasks such as handling repeat orders along a supply chain from manufacturer to retailer. B2C applications allow customers to complete automated transactions. This is good stuff for e-commerce, but it's not exactly what we mean when we talk about relationships in public relations. What are more critical to public relations are the forms of human communication that go along with these technologies.

General-access Web pages and discussion forums, intranets, extranets, consumer-generated media, and plain old e-mail cover a range of technologies from the broadest levels of mass commerce to the most personalized forms of commerce-driven communication between an organization and its publics.

Commerce-driven Web pages. Stuart Esrock and Greg Leichty (2000) were among the first to take a serious look at how profitable organizations were using Web pages for public relations purposes. They studied Fortune 500 company Web sites in 1997 and again in 1999 and found, not surprisingly, that these companies tailored their Web content for the press, investors, customers, and prospective employees among other publics (Esrock & Leichty, 2000). They inferred, quite logically, that the prominence of materials on a company's home page indicated the primary publics the site was designed to reach. If press releases were front and center on the home page, Esrock and Leichty figured news media were a primary public. As you might have expected, this emphasis on news was most common in the 1997 study. However, by the second wave of the study in 1999, the researchers observed something different. Relative to investors, customers, and potential employees, the press was a secondary public, at least in terms of the structure of the organizations' front pages. The media relations functions of these Web sites didn't disappear; they just moved backstage a bit.

Esrock and Leichty (2000) seem to have uncovered a lasting lesson in a changing media environment. Almost a decade later, as podcasts and executive blogs like those posted by General Motors and Sun Microsystems became the focus of "cutting-edge" seminars and public relations agency tip sheets Web-wide, *New York Times* journalist John Markoff told the public relations trade publication *Bulldog Reporter* the following: "Reporters really don't find that much use in [blogs]. Their real value is in being a direct channel to the public" (as cited in Pittman, 2005). Not all reporters would agree with Markoff, but the take-home point stands that Web-based public relations clearly extends directly to "the public" (or "publics," as strategic public relations people see them) beyond the news media.

Of course, Fortune 500 companies have large public relations staffs or large public relations agency teams at their service, but even large public relations teams are greatly outnumbered by the number of people they hope their organization will communicate with beyond traditional mass media. This begs the question of how public relations teams ranging anywhere from 2 to 20 in size can carry on conversational communication with so many niche media, customers, consumers, investors, and donors.

How can public relations efforts be distributed online? Part of the answer still lies in the one-to-many tactics of old-fashioned corporate communication. Just as effective media relations require stepping into the shoes of journalists, effective consumer relations, investor relations, donor relations, and employee relations mean taking the perspective of the consumers, investors, donors, and employees who visit you online.

General-access facts and frequently asked questions. When done right, these offer people facts and information they actually want.

Are the frequently asked questions (FAQ) really asked frequently?

For some reason, my home address won't register on the Web page for one of the national pizza chains in my town. I enter my quirky order online (using a coupon for two free toppings, but asking for four toppings on half and just cheese on the other half). I figure this will be a lot easier to get right online than it will be to negotiate with the harried guy who answers the phone. But then when I try to submit the order, my address won't register. So I have to call anyhow. I ask the guy on the phone why my address works on his computer but not mine.

92   PUBLIC RELATIONS ONLINE

He has no idea. The delivery driver doesn't know either. So before I try to order from them again, I check the FAQ page.

There was a time when I would expect to find on the FAQ page answers to trivia-type questions like when the company was founded and how many pounds of pizza dough they use in a day. But I am now thankful that as consumer-targeted Web pages have improved, the likelihood of finding the answer to my question in FAQ sections has increased. The Domino's Pizza FAQ page includes, "Can you help me with online ordering?" and Papa John's has an online customer feedback form that specifically asks if my feedback is related to online ordering.

In doing my "research" for this chapter, I went ahead and filled out the Papa John's customer feedback form. In a few minutes I got an e-mail from one of their employees:

Tom

I do apologize for the inconvenience, however Online Ordering is currently unavailable for your address. Our current US Postal Service information indicates your address is invalid. Some possible explanations for this may be: new construction, recent change of street name or number, or new zip code. Please feel free to check back for future updates. Until then, Ordering Online will be unavailable.

Evan
Consumer Services Team

This works for me. The new-construction explanation makes sense where I live. I doubt Evan's job description includes the actual words *public relations*, but his function on the Consumer Services Team is certainly part of his company's relationship with its publics. If he offers me a cynical answer or ignores my request, and if I were the type to get vocal about my pizza mishaps, I might go and blog about it, or go complain on the forum at http://www.papajohnsucks.com/—yes, it's a real page.[1] Then there would be no question of whether this is a public relations issue. (We will look at this from the perspective of http://www.pizzadeliverydrivers.org/ in the next chapter.)

Online forums. Because there is a huge gap between the types of questions that are asked so often that they belong within a click or two of an organization's home page and the questions that require one-to-one attention, many organizations host online forums with searchable archives.

For example, if you've got a fairly specific question about your computer hardware, there is a pretty good chance someone else using that hardware has the same question, such as "Will my Hewlett Packard 4110 OfficeJet printer work with my Apple Airport Extreme?" We probably wouldn't call this a "frequently asked" question, but even if it's asked a couple of times, the organization can save time by making the answer available to anyone who looks for it in the future.

This isn't a question to post prominently to www.hp.com or www .apple.com, but it's also not the type of question that Hewlett Packard (HP) and Apple should have to rewrite an individual response for every time it is asked. This is how online forums are useful. For example, a forum may be set up for people with questions for HP about the OfficeJet 4100 line of printers. First you can do a search to see if the question already has been answered. If you don't have any luck, then you can ask the question yourself. When a tech person answers, she can then archive that answer so it shows up for the next person who might search for it.

For this whole process of answering questions and adapting to the business environment to work, the gears of internal communication must be oiled well. This is why public relations people should be involved. On the surface, these are issues of marketing, information technology (IT), and store management, but handling them requires both smooth internal communication and effective external communication. Otherwise, those communicating on behalf of an organization—including pizza order takers and consumer hardware technicians—will find themselves unable to keep up with questions, or offering answers like, "I don't know" and "That's just what the computer is telling me."

Public relations people cannot possibly do it all, but they can work to distribute the function of building and maintaining relationships between an organization and its online publics among internal and external groups. This is where server-side, one-to-many communication starts to look more like peer-to-peer, many-to-many communication.

We find social concepts and technological concepts running parallel yet again as we turn our attention to intranets and extranets as technologies that aid communication among internal and external groups.

Intranets and extranets. Intranets allow a business to keep some information semi-private. Privacy doesn't mean sinister secrecy. It just means employees and members can share information such as their home contact information, proprietary business ideas, benefits concerns, and even goofy photos from the company picnic with their colleagues without worrying too much about this information flowing out to the public domain. Of course, some information might "leak" out,

94   PUBLIC RELATIONS ONLINE

and it is possible that an outsider could hack into an intranet, so we can't say that intranet communication is completely worry free, but intranets do afford internal publics at least the general expectation that access to the content will be limited to colleagues in the same organization. Intranets are particularly helpful in geographically dispersed organizations, adding an additional communication channel to help people in distant locations build and maintain more productive working relationships (Hallahan, 2004).

Public relations people can participate in intranets to keep in touch with issues important to internal publics, which again is a big part of the boundary-spanning role. They also can use intranets to distribute information internally. In other words, systems, server-side, and peer-to-peer public relations tactics all can be used to build and maintain online relationships with internal publics such as employees, members, and volunteers.

Whereas intranets are designed for internal publics, extranets serve external publics such as vendors, credentialed news media, and even public relations agency clients. Marketing data, inventory lists, breaking news releases, and updated media lists might be shared among select internal and external groups. In promoting Ogilvy Public Relations Worldwide's expertise in online communication, senior vice president John Bell (n.d.) described his agency's use of extranets as follows:

> With our collaborative extranets, we can share material across borders instantly. We can manage a far-flung team, carry on online dialogue, and deliver relevant news streams right to the desktop. Our Communications Central extranet has a component approach to give agency and client teammates the right "dashboard" for any engagement.

Consumer-generated media (CGM). CGM is yet another set of initials to describe online communication forms that include blogs, ratings sites, rogue Web sites (e.g., www.papajohnsucks.com), podcasts, and the like. Whereas we might think of Fortune 500 Web pages, FAQ pages, product discussion forums, intranets, and extranets as pretty much owned by the organizations that host them, the term *CGM* suggests a different kind of ownership. Even if the topic is your organization's products or services, you will have no more control over the conversation than you would if it were happening in an Italian café or Taipei noodle house.

As Pete Blackshaw (2005) said, "CGM can be influenced, but not controlled, by marketers." Blackshaw, a columnist on digital marketing strategies for JupiterMedia's ClickZ network, gets at a lasting media concept that should be familiar to anyone studying public relations: the continuum between highly controlled media such as paid advertisements and highly uncontrolled media such as the content of an editorial page (see also Questionable Claims in Chapter 6). CGM, such as blogs, ratings sites, third-party discussion forums, podcasts, and so forth, obviously fall on the uncontrolled side of the spectrum from a marketer's perspective. But from another perspective, as media relations expert Lloyd P. Trufelman put it in a 2005 *Public Relations Tactics* article, "Media *consumers* are exhibiting much *more control* over the content they receive" (p. 17, italics added). One group's loss of control may be another's gain. From the consumer's perspective, this is the beauty of CGM. To understand the array of perspectives in online communication, we must take into account the people using the technologies.

People and the Cultures of Online Commerce

Working to understand the perspectives of individuals in the context of unique cultures is not a new idea in business-driven communication, but one that was amplified with the "de-massification" of media in the late 20th century. The concept of *integrated marketing communication* offers lasting ideas that help us make sense of why and how individuals make use of the constantly changing communication technologies that are central to online commerce.

In the big picture of two-way communication between organizations and publics, computers were first used in gathering information much more than they were in disseminating it. In the early 1970s, General Electric (GE) developed a theory called Focus that was built on the idea that "all good advertising begins with a fundamental understanding of the receiver," according to professor and former GE marketing executive Bob Lauterborn (as cited in Schultz, Tannenbaum, & Lauterborn, 1993, pp. 6–7). And with increased marketer access to computers and databases in the 1990s, the idea became "implementable" (p. 11). Lauterborn (as cited in Schultz et al., 1993) converted the four Ps of marketing—product, price, place, and promotion—to the four Cs—consumer wants and needs, costs to satisfy those wants and needs, convenience to buy, and communication. "The motto of the age of the manufacturer—*caveat emptor,* let the buyer beware—is replaced by *caveat emptorum,* beware of the buyer" (as cited in Schultz et al., 1993, p. 13).

Rapid rises in rates of consumer access to computer-mediated communication technology trailed the trends in marketers' access to computing technologies by only a few years, and two-way models of

96   PUBLIC RELATIONS ONLINE

communication took off further from there. Schultz et al. (1993) placed consumer perceptions at the heart of their concept of integrated marketing communication. This means that the real "integration" of brands happens in the consumer's views and experiences, even more so than in the flowcharts of organizations aspiring to espouse those brand ideals. My perceptions of the Papa John's brand is based on the gestalt of my experience with their ads, their pizzas (and the pepperoncinis they put next to the pizzas), their Web site, their delivery drivers, my conversations with the people who answer the phones, what I have read on www.papajohnsucks.com, the e-mail Evan sent me, and every other point of contact I have had with the organization.

Public relations, marketing, advertising, IT, human resources (HR), and every other part of an organization that comes into contact with the organization's publics play a role in the way consumers see the organization. This brings to mind van Ruler's (2004) conductor-type from Chapter 3. Although public relations people should work to understand all these points of contact, they should be especially involved in the processes of communication when identifying consumer wants and needs.

Employees and internal publics. One of the simplest ways to segment publics in business environments is to distinguish between internal and external publics. Once you have determined whether a public is internal or external given the circumstances, you can take into account how organizational cultures affect employees and members when they are involved in online communication between the organization and its publics.

During crises, internal communication becomes more important than ever. Maintaining a first-person sense of "we" is one of the few things that can help pull an organization through tough times, and online media can offer a way for top management to stay in touch with internal publics while also responding to the tremendous external demands of government and media.

During and following the attacks of September 11, 2001, American Airlines made use of a number of internal channels, including an intranet, employee e-mail, fax-on-demand, and electronic newsletters. Joe Downing's (2004) case study of American Airlines' use of mediated communication during that massive crisis was cited in Chapter 2 as an example of how the different faces of American Airlines' online presence serve different roles from a systems view, with a major Web site devoted to consumers and another intranet reserved for internal communication. Perhaps the most telling part of the case, however, was how a campaign called Good Words evolved. American Airlines' manager of employee communication Mick Doherty and his colleagues started the effort on September 24 to pass along to internal publics the words of condolence, prayers, and poems that they had received. They interspersed these pieces in with the troubling operational news they had to deliver daily via e-mail, the intranet, and other channels. Then something interesting happened.

> Employees began to send in their own stories, and these were added to the messages the airline had already received. Ultimately, this allowed employee reactions to become part of the story. (Downing, 2004, p. 45)

As more employees read the communication, more also submitted their own stories. Doherty (as cited in Downing, 2004, p. 45) described the communication as "self-replicating." This goes to show how internal communication can work when online media are seen as "our" media rather than someone else's. It also shows how organizational culture is not something defined and distributed by top management in a server-side process from few to many, but something developed in a peer-to-peer exchange among members of the various groups involved. The role of public relations became less about targeting messages and more about inviting internal publics to a conversation and encouraging them to bring their own thoughts and feelings to the table, thereby sharing experiences and building an environment, rather than just receiving a message.

Questions of how culture is communicated online and to what effect are also at the center of consumer relations concerns, especially in a worldwide context.

Consumers and customers. "Globalization simultaneously creates tendencies toward some degree of cultural (structural) homogenization while at the same time it encourages people to identify more strongly with their ethnic or national grouping," say researchers Michael Maynard and Yan Tian (2004). This statement outlines the foundation for a sophisticated approach to communicating with consumers and customers in an online environment, in which posting new material to a Web page in Atlanta carries the risk of putting off a huge group of people in Beijing. Maynard and Tian call it "glocalization" when global companies with global brands such as Coca Cola design Web presences from local perspectives.

Of course, there are countless cultures even in the metro Atlanta area to take into account. You need not travel far—virtually or otherwise—to be overwhelmed by the diversity of perspectives to consider

98   PUBLIC RELATIONS ONLINE

in supporting even a single local brand. This is why one-size-fits-all marketing is so limited. The trick is to find the right balance between two extremes. Trying to be all things to all people doesn't make much sense because your organization will have no consistent identity (i.e., brand)—no one, not even you, will know what your company is all about. On the other hand, a totally homogenous and stagnant "company line" of communication designed to appeal to the broadest possible market likely will end up bland and generic, which also misses the point of online communication. Stagnant systems don't adapt.

So what's the solution? "Since corporations and businesses aren't individuals, ultimately their authenticity is rooted in their employees. . . . When a conversation is required, or even just desired, being able to count upon a rich range of corporate spokespeople is crucial" (Searls & Weinberger, 2001, pp. 100, 110). Whenever your company's employees speak online in the first-person voice, they are spokespeople for the organization. They contribute to the environment, experiences, and even the internal thoughts and feelings of your publics. But they act as eyes and ears too in the process of two-way communication.

We might call this *distributed public relations.* With an immediate nod to Dan Gillmor (2005) for his work with the concept of "distributed journalism," a definition of "distributed public relations" might be in order:

> **distributed public relations:** *n.* intentional practice of sharing public relations responsibilities among a broad cross-section of an organization's members or employees, particularly in an online context.

Open conversations yield good data to help understand customers and other publics. Talk with employees to see what they have learned about the diversity of customer perspectives out there. Collaborate with all the people who come into online contact with your company's customers. Avoid turf battles. Get involved in the conversations too so you can speak directly with consumers and customers.

The general idea here is to realize that different groups of consumers have different interests, and it is possible to work those interests into your business model while at the same time communicating out about your products and services. Shel Holtz (1999), for example, explains how public relations people can work with IT people to achieve some harmony in online communication, profit driven or otherwise:

Sit down with your IT counterparts and discuss your objectives. IT needs to understand what you are trying to accomplish on the company's behalf and how the intranet and/or Web figure into the equation. Listen to IT's objectives. With all your cards on the table, take that next big step: Agree to work together to provide the solutions the organization needs in order to be successful and competitive. (p. 252)

This type of conversation can work just as well with marketing, advertising, and other departments that are attuned to consumer wants and needs. And for financial publics such as investors and analysts, you can extend this model of cooperation to investor relations (IR).

Investors. In the 1990s and early 2000s, large brokerage firms such as Morgan Stanley Dean Witter and Merrill Lynch had to adapt to the demand for a more individualized trading environment, which was brought about by the services of do-it-yourself online discount brokerages like E*Trade (Kawamoto, 2003). The shift from big brokerages doing almost all of the business to individual investors making more individual trades online mirrors de-massification trends in other industries.

Online, public relations and IR can work together to make sure that financial information is available whenever appropriate and that this information is presented in a form that is easily accessible by all interested parties, including individual investors. The two departments can work together with IT and even HR (if, say, stock options are part of employee benefits packages), to make sure the organization's financial records are available when they should be and in line with the requirements of regulatory agencies such as the Securities and Exchange Commission in the United States.

Donors. Dot-orgs need investors as much as dot-coms. Nonprofit organizations must compete with other organizations to convince donors that money donated constitutes a wise investment. Although the return on that investment may be disaster relief, disease control and prevention, education programs, or reforestation efforts, getting those efforts funded can be just as competitive—if not more so—than convincing people that a company's stock will pay dividends. Online media offer new opportunities to identify and cultivate relationships with potential investors and donors supporting social and environmental issues. Chapter 8 looks at online relationships when the context of online public relations is as much a marketplace of ideas as it is a marketplace of commerce.

100   PUBLIC RELATIONS ONLINE

Questionable Claims

❖ NONE OF OUR BUSINESS?

XBRL (extensible business reporting language) is a good example of the intersection between online technologies and the interests of financial publics. XBRL is based on the same technology as RSS (really simple syndication). Like HTML (hypertext mark-up language), it allows people entering and reporting data from a wide variety of organizations using different computer platforms to present data in a consistent format. That way, a potential investor could analyze the financial documents of several companies in the same industry without having to manually thumb through piles of documents distributed by each organization to make apples-to-apples comparisons. For example, net profit is tagged the same way for every company using XBRL, so an investor easily can download and compare net profits between multiple companies.

Companies can use this technology to make it easier to update public information such as the contents of quarterly and annual reports. XBRL is designed to make it easier for companies in the United States to comply with the disclosure standards of the Securities and Exchange Commission (SEC). It makes it easier for companies to file annual and quarterly reports to the SEC's EDGAR (Electronic Data Gathering and Retrieval) database. The finance-phobic public relations practitioner may ask, "Is that really something I need to worry about?"

XBRL is as commerce driven as any communication technology out there, but it is also helping public relations people in their efforts to establish more transparency. Even though it is tempting to write off such technologies as the domain of another department, Michelle Savage (2005), vice president of IR for PR Newswire makes a compelling argument for public relations practitioners to get involved. What's at stake, according to Savage, is the idea that "all of a company's critical audiences can access news and financial information" (p. 12). Whether this happens from the full adoption of XBRL or some other technology, the importance of public relations people understanding how financial information gets communicated is critical.

❖ NOTE

1. The site provider "closed" the site on August 16, 2005, and stopped adding new content.

❖ REFERENCES

Bell, J. (n.d.). *Expertise: Internet communications.* Retrieved June 14, 2006, from http://www.ogilvypr.com/expertise/internet-communications.cfm

Blackshaw, P. (2005, June 28). *The pocket guide to consumer generated media.* Retrieved June 14, 2006, from http://www.clickz.com/experts/brand/cmo/article.php/3515576

Downing, J. R. (2004). American Airlines' use of mediated employee channels after the 9/11 attacks. *Public Relations Review, 30,* 37–48.

Esrock, S. L., & Leichty, G. B. (2000). Organization of corporate Web pages: Publics and functions. *Public Relations Review, 26,* 327–344.

Gillmor, D. (2005, January 5). *Distributed journalism's future.* Retrieved June 14, 2006, from http://dangillmor.typepad.com/dan_gillmor_on_grass roots/2005/01/distributed_jou.html

Hallahan, K. (2004). Online public relations. In Hossein Bidgoli (Ed.), *The Internet encyclopedia* (Vol. 2, pp. 769–783). Hoboken, NJ: John Wiley.

Holtz, S. (1999). *Public relations on the Net: Winning strategies to inform and influence the media, the investment community, the public, and more!* New York: AMACOM.

Kawamoto, K. (2003). *Media and society in the digital age.* Boston: Allyn & Bacon.

Maynard, M., & Tian, Y. (2004). Between global and glocal: Content analysis of the Chinese Web sites of the 100 top global brands. *Public Relations Review, 30,* 285–291.

O'Brien, K. (2005, June 16). *PRWeek.com exclusive: PR and the "long tail."* Retrieved July 6, 2005, from http://www.prweek.com/news/news_ story_free.cfm?ID=238966&site=3

Pittman, B. (2005, July 7). Tech tools no substitute for old-school media relations, says *NYT* scribe—Three tips to help put wikis, blogs and podcasts into perspective. In B. Pittman (Ed.), *Journalists speak out on PR* (E-mail newsletter). Emeryville, CA: Infocom Group.

Savage, M. (2005). Why you need to understand XBRL. *PR Strategist, 11*(1), 10–12.

Schultz, D. E., Tannenbaum, S. I., & Lauterborn, R. F. (1993). *Integrated marketing communications.* Lincolnwood, IL: NTC Business Books.

Searls, D., & Weinberger, D. (2001). Markets are conversations. In R. Levine, C. Locke, D. Searls, & D. Weinberger (Eds.), *The cluetrain manifesto: The end of business as usual* (pp. 75–114). New York: Perseus.

Trufelman, L. P. (2005, May). Consumer-generated media—Challenges and opportunities for public relations. *Public Relations Tactics, 12*(5), 17, 27.

van Ruler, B. (2004). The communication grid: An introduction of a model of four communication strategies. *Public Relations Review, 30,* 123–143.

102   PUBLIC RELATIONS ONLINE

Hands-Online Activity

❖ DO-IT-YOURSELF FAQ TIPS

   1. Revisit some commercial Web sites that you have used in the past few weeks and find at least two examples of FAQs from these sites. For example, if you ordered a pizza online, you might go to http://www.pizzahut.com/ and from there find http://www.pizzahut.com/faq/.

     a. URL for first FAQ _____
     b. URL for second FAQ _____

   2. This chapter offers some advice for writing FAQs from the perspective of those using the Web sites. Two tips are listed here for writing FAQs that support relationships between organizations doing business online and the publics who will make or break the success of that business. Working from the previous URLs, note examples (good or bad) of FAQ items that illustrate these ideas.

     Tip 1: Ensure that your frequently asked questions really are asked frequently.

Example of a FAQ that you think really is asked frequently (or one that you think almost never gets asked):

     Tip 2: Be conversational. This means being responsive in tone as well as making contact information available if the customer needs more information than you offer in your FAQ.

Example of a conversational FAQ item (or a particularly non-conversational one):

3. Write three tips of your own and add examples to illustrate what you mean.

Tip 3:

Example:

Tip 4:

Example:

Tip 5:

Example:

8

Issue-Driven Relationships

Connecting everyone (on the Net) to everyone (on the Net) has made the world a smaller place by breaking down geographical barriers. It has not, however, enabled everyone to work with everyone else!

—Tim Berners-Lee (2005)

❖ OVERVIEW

Online, any group can organize into an "organization," and any organization might be considered a "public." Whether people can even access online media, their individual activity online if they do have access, and the power in numbers of social networks and formal alliances are all covered as antecedents to issue-driven public relations online. Common features of activist and nonprofit Web pages are discussed. The promise of the Internet to serve as a tool for relationship building and productive social discussion is discussed along with the Internet's capacity as a hotbed for malice and misinformation.

106   PUBLIC RELATIONS ONLINE

❖ ISSUES AND ONLINE ORGANIZATIONS AND PUBLICS

This chapter looks at how online media work in an environment in which any group can organize into an "organization" and any organization might be considered a "public." Grunig and Hunt (1984) have suggested that one of the defining features of a public is a common issue of concern to all its members. Issues are socially defined and normally brought to our attention by people advocating for one side or another. That Microsoft generated more revenues than any other software company in 2005 (and 2004, and 2003 . . .) is not disputed—it's more of a fact than an "issue." But whether Microsoft is a good corporate citizen is often debated—that's a socially defined *issue.* People working for Microsoft, particularly in public relations–related functions, might argue that Microsoft is "doing good by doing well." Microsoft critics, such as the Project to Promote Competition and Innovation in the Digital Age (www.procompetition.org), make arguments that Microsoft does more harm than good in the competitive business environment. Both sides are advocating in the online marketplace of ideas. Issues most often involve disputes about fairness, security, or environmental concerns (Hallahan, 2001; Heath, 1997).

In the last chapter, we looked at big pizza businesses as organizations, and we approached activists posting to sites like www .papajohnsucks.com as publics. In this chapter, we might think of the people behind www.pizzadeliverydrivers.org or www.procompetition .org as organizations, with corporations like Domino's and Microsoft as their publics. Indeed, www.pizzadeliverydrivers.org represents an effort by pizza delivery drivers to organize into a labor union to gain power in the relationship.

Among critical scholars in public relations—those studying the balance of power in relationships between organizations and their publics—some have seen the Internet as a "potential equalizer," or a place where the virtual playing field between the relatively powerful and the relatively powerless may start to be leveled somewhat (Coombs, 1998; Heath, 1998). The word *potential* is an especially important qualifier in this context.

❖ WHAT NEEDS TO BE IN PLACE?

As with news-driven and commerce-driven relationships, issue-driven relationships among online organizations and online publics depend on the technology and content of online communication, the individual people involved, and the networks people form online.

Technology and Content

Discussions in the previous two chapters on media relations and e-commerce were based on the assumption that most working news media and most investors and customers with discretionary income have access to Internet technologies. When it comes to communication about issues, however, we have to be a lot more careful in assuming that publics have access to online media content. The potential for the Internet to level the field between the haves and have-nots is very much dependent on the idea that everyone involved has a voice in cyberspace. Scientific and philosophical debates about the "digital divide" have underscored this point. Although some argue that Internet-related technologies are social equalizers, others argue the opposite—that people and societies with access to information technologies are advancing further as a result of these technologies, whereas those without access are falling further behind.

In any case, the first question for people considering online public relations is whether the organization and its publics even have access to and are willing to use the channels of online communication. In all likelihood, the fact that you are even reading a book on the topic of online public relations means you can access the Internet with a few taps of your fingers. Public relations people must be careful, however, not to assume that all—or even most—of the people they should communicate with are online. Many of the most important global challenges in public relations are about communication among people who do not have access to the Internet.

Many may not even have proxy voices online. For example, public relations critic Mohan J. Dutta-Bergman (2005) at Purdue University examined the political economies of the Philippines, Chile, and Nicaragua to call into question how well public relations can really serve the interests of those with no access to even the most basic media technologies. He reminds us that the interests of people living in "marginalized spaces of the world" are not necessarily served by public relations tactics of the "transnational elite" (p. 267). Although such criticism doesn't make for light reading, it highlights the bitter contrast between the promise of Internet-based international public relations as an equalizing force with the economic reality that much of the world does not participate in online marketplaces, or even marketplaces of ideas as we know them in more developed countries.

108   PUBLIC RELATIONS ONLINE

Nonetheless, many individuals—ranging from people opening free e-mail accounts at public library computer terminals to Silicon Valley entrepreneurs who have earned wealth and influence for their roles in pioneering online media—are using the Internet as a landscape for new types of negotiation. The topography of this landscape differs markedly from the even-more-limited-access, even-more-expensive world of communication via mass media such as network TV and high-circulation print media. New players step foot on this landscape every hour. Many find ways to make their voices heard louder than ever before. The tables presented later in this chapter show how issue-driven organizations have access to many of the same online tools for presenting information as the commerce-driven organizations discussed in the Technology and Content section of Chapter 7. In most cases, access to the Internet marketplace of ideas comes much cheaper and easier than access to the mass media marketplace of commerce.

The lack of systematic editorial controls that people might expect from traditional mass media means organizations and publics of all sorts can publish news and facts online with minimal checks on veracity. This can be especially problematic when communicators remain anonymous because reputation and credibility become less effective as controls. Whereas crooks and terrorists use easy access and anonymity to cover their tracks and elude laws, those managing legitimate marketplaces of commerce (e.g., eBay, Amazon) and marketplaces of ideas (e.g., Wikipedia, Slashdot) have pioneered new systems of balancing easy access with concerns for reliability and veracity. eBay's "feedback" system and Slashdot's "karma" are evolving forms of reputation management in these evolving forms of online communities.

Individuals—Putting the Active in Interactive Media

In the late 1990s and early 2000s, several U.S.-based authors and scholars started to look at what online media meant for public relations, issues management, and activism (e.g., Coombs, 1998; Esrock & Leichty, 1998; Heath, 1998; Taylor, Kent, & White, 2001). In an effort to get a handle on how this initial flurry of U.S.-based inquiry into the effects of online communication might apply elsewhere, Elizabeth Dougall, Andrew Fox, and Lorelle Burton (2001) surveyed Australian public relations practitioners to learn how computer-mediated communication (CMC) was changing the way they communicated. The results of the survey showed that these practitioners generally agreed in principle with most of the main tenets of growing bodies of scholarly and professional literature on online public relations. This snapshot captured some lasting ideas about the way public relations people feel about online media that appear to generalize across borders and, so far, across the years since the study was conducted:

- Online media offer more opportunities for public relations practitioners to engage in two-way communication and broader dialogue between organizations and publics.
- The landscape of online communication is volatile. Respondents "strongly supported the contention that special interest groups wield more power in the on-line environment and agree that CMC makes it even harder to control what is being said about their organizations" (Dougall, Fox, & Burton, 2001, p. 29).
- Online media are important tools in issues management.
- Online media will continue to grow in importance for public relations, but offline communication channels are still of paramount importance.

Given that individual public relations practitioners see the importance of online media, a logical next question is how people who may or may not think of themselves as public relations practitioners get engaged in online communication between organizations and publics.

Public relations–specific research on what gets people to step up and become active members of publics has benefited from James Grunig's (1997) situational theory of publics. Basically, this theory suggests that people range from being members of latent publics to being members of active publics based on levels of problem recognition, constraint recognition, and involvement. People who meet the following criteria are more likely to take action, or become members of active publics: (a) high problem recognition—they see an issue as a problem and get concerned, (b) low constraint recognition—they feel like they can actually do something about the problem, and (c) high involvement—they see the problem as relevant to their own lives.

Although situational theory helps us understand the processes by which individual people change their communication behaviors, what makes it important to online public relations is how it provides a foundation for understanding the formation of networks of like-minded people who are motivated and able to take action using online media.

Active Social Networks

Getting organized to take a stand on an issue historically has been easier for people working in established organizations such as the U.S.

110   PUBLIC RELATIONS ONLINE

Environmental Protection Agency (EPA) or multinational corporations such as ExxonMobil. With budgets to contract for public relations campaigns, such organizations have been executing strategic public relations for decades, if not centuries. Edward Bernays's work in 1930 to promote cigarettes to women is a classic example (Cutlip, 1994). Bernays, hired by the American Tobacco Company to promote Lucky Strikes cigarettes to women, worked behind the scenes to orchestrate a publicity stunt in which 10 of New York City's debutants marched down Fifth Avenue in an Easter parade while flaunting their "torches of freedom" (Cutlip, 1994, p. 210). Armed with psychoanalytic ideas about the social oppression of women, and basic market demographics showing that about half (the female half) of the U.S. market for cigarettes was yet to be tapped, Bernays provided historians a classic example of the power of public relations to alter social definitions. According to Bernays, the campaign was a success in breaking down the taboo of women smoking in public. What was absent from Bernays's environment, however, were online anti-tobacco groups and bloggers working to uncover and report the connection between torches of freedom, Lucky Strikes, Edward Bernays, and the American Tobacco Company.

Fast forward to the early years of this millennium. Log on to the Web and type in a keyword search for *tobacco issue* or *environmental issue* or even *pizza delivery issue*. I just did the last one for kicks and the first result—the I'm-feeling-lucky return from Google—was an essay by economics professor Thomas J. DiLorenzo (1997) entitled *Life, Liberty, and Pizza Delivery*, in which Dominos' policy of not delivering pizzas in neighborhoods that it has deemed too dangerous for its drivers is framed as a civil rights issue for pizza-craving people in those high-crime neighborhoods.

Finding publics and organizations clashing over more traditional issues online is just as easy. For example, Public Employees for Environmental Responsibility (PEER, http://www.peer.org) and the Stop ExxonMobil Alliance (http://www.stopexxonmobil.org) are at the forefront of online opposition to the public relations tactics of the EPA and ExxonMobil, respectively.

In 2005, the EPA was called to task in the *New York Times* for contracting public relations help:

WASHINGTON, July 17—The Office of Research and Development at the Environmental Protection Agency is seeking outside public relations consultants, to be paid up to $5 million over five years, to polish its Web site, organize focus groups on how to buff the office's image and ghostwrite articles "for publication in scholarly journals and magazines." (Barringer, 2005, pp. A1, A16)

It appears PEER provided the tip for the story:

"The idea that they would take limited science dollars and spend them on P.R. is not only ill advised, it's just plain stupid," [PEER director Jeff] Ruch said in an interview. (Barringer, 2005, pp. A1, 16)

Similarly, ExxonMobil was the focus for A-list liberal blogger Markos Moulitsas Zúniga, who posted a biting critique of ExxonMobil in his Daily Kos blog for the "funding of think tanks, religious groups, media outlets and other organizations, to spread doubt about the reality of global climate change" (2005). His source? StopExxonMobil.org.

Although the arteries running through both these critiques are the money trails leading to powerful institutions, the network-supported public relations tactics executed by StopExxonMobil and PEER reveal how Bernays's idea of the "engineering of consent," particularly by way of building alliances, is not the exclusive domain of blue-chip corporations and well-heeled government agencies. StopExxonMobil lists the following organizations as members of its alliance that are "dedicated to committing ExxonMobil to socially responsible behavior":

- Alliance for Democracy: www.thealliancefordemocracy.org
- Amnesty International USA: www.amnesty-usa.org
- Free the Planet: www.freetheplanet.org
- Greenpeace: www.greenpeaceusa.org, www.exxonsecrets.org, www.dontbuyexxonmobil.org
- Institute for Policy Studies: www.seen.org
- International Labor Rights Fund: www.laborrights.org
- Pacific Environment: www.pacificenvironment.org
- PressurePoint: www.pressurepoint.org
- Refinery Reform Campaign: www.refineryreform.org
- Students for a Free Tibet: www.studentsforafreetibet.org
- Uproar: www.uproarnow.org
- U.S. Public Interest Research Group: www.uspirg.org

Ironically, many of the very tactics criticized by organizations such as PEER and StopExxonMobil are the ones these organizations are applying themselves. By banding together like-minded people and like-minded organizations, they're fighting fire with fire, and online media are fueling the flames.

112   PUBLIC RELATIONS ONLINE

❖ SHIFTING FROM ACTIVE PUBLICS
TO ACTIVE ORGANIZATIONS

Juliet Roper (2002) at the University of Waikato in New Zealand analyzed 150 Web sites that she selected based on their global scope and
their activist nature. She found that activist organizations were using
the Internet as a tool to gain power in public policy discussions, with
publics shifting their roles from being "consumers" to being "citizens."
According to Roper, as consumers, people are influenced by corporations directly. Corporations also influence people indirectly when corporations affect public policy. "The dominant corporate view here,
supported by governments, is that individuals are dependent upon
business for products, jobs, and welfare" (Roper, 2002, p. 115). When
people take the role of citizens, however, the pattern of influence can
get turned on its head. Publics "reassert their political primacy and
governments, in turn, reassert legislative power" (Roper, 2002, p. 122).

So how exactly do active publics use the Internet to pull off such a
shift? Roper found that organization and information are critical.

Organization. This one word really sums up a shift in perspectives
from a public as a target for some other organization to a public as an
organized entity in itself—an organization. Networking, strategy coor-
dination, and training are all part of the process of organizing online.
Networking brings groups together—sometimes groups of groups—to
build a large alliance of people ready to take action. That action often
comes in the form of mass e-mail campaigns or other coordinated tactics to demonstrate the magnitude of concern over an issue to legislators or other decision makers. The major result of such organizing and
alliance building is that organizations construct the "capability of generating mass responses to events and policies that might otherwise
have passed unnoticed" (Roper, 2002, p. 119).

Information. Information is power in this context. Research conducted and gathered by organizational members helps active publics
gain power in policy discussions. For example, GE Free, a New Zealand
alliance opposing genetic engineering, used its Web site to provide
unmediated information to constituents. The information included international opinion surveys, scientific reports, and information about field
trials of genetically engineered crops in other parts of the world. The campaign was "highly successful in raising public awareness of the issues
involved and gaining public support for a GE free stance" (Henderson,
2005, p. 129). Organizations also commonly post campaign development
materials (media lists, sample news releases, fact sheets, tutorials on
how to conduct research, etc.) online for their members to use.

Issue-Driven Relationships   113

Kang and Norton (2004) explored how a sample of 100 large non-profit organizations were using the Web. The authors used a 2001 list of the largest U.S. nonprofit organizations to draw the sample. Typical content for these pages included mission statements, press releases, policy issue statements, and community service information (see Tables 8.1 and 8.2). Many nonprofits also included information about social responsibility and speeches from the organizations' top leaders.

❖ RELATIONAL GOALS AND OUTCOMES

When it came to including features that Kang and Norton (2004) called "interactive," fewer Web sites had the goods. Less than 10% included discussion forums, chat rooms, online polls, or online surveys. Of course, the top 100 nonprofits in the United States make for a far different sample than organizations normally classified as "activists." Taylor et al. (2001) sampled 100 Web sites hosted by organizations that they defined as activist. Tables 8.1, 8.2, and 8.3 highlight some of the similarities and differences in the ways these two different categories of organizations were using their Web sites shortly after the turn of the millennium.

The relative lack of large U.S. nonprofits using the Web to promote alliances with other nonprofits suggests a different type of online positioning for these organizations. Only 8% of the big U.S. nonprofits linked to other similar organizations. Their goals for relationship building might be different than smaller but more global alliances that rely more on each other to gain power in numbers.

Relationships in alliances. Of the relational strategies discussed in Chapter 5, social networks and task sharing stand out as especially important strategies for building trust, satisfaction, and commitment, which are key relational outcomes in organizations and in alliances. For the nonprofits, we might infer the importance of these factors from Kang and Norton's (2004) findings on the prominence of contact information, details on how to become affiliated with the organization, information on how to donate money, information request functions, online forms allowing people to join the organization, and links to local branches (all included on more than half the nonprofit Web pages).

For the broader population of activist organizations discussed by Henderson (2005) and Taylor et al. (2001), the prominence of cross-linking among activist organizations, ways to contact political leaders, and member-base rosters offer evidence of social networks and task sharing as common relational strategies. What brings these diverse alliances together is a common stance on issues.

114   PUBLIC RELATIONS ONLINE

Table 8.1   Common Items Tallied by Both Kang and Norton (2004) and
                     Taylor et al. (2001)

Kang and Norton's (2004) Characteristics of Largest U.S. Nonprofit Organizations' Web Sites	Taylor et al.'s (2001) Occurrence of Dialogic Features on 100 Activist Web Sites
Details on how to become affiliated (98%)	Details on how to become affiliated (91%)
Logos and icons (95%)	Prominent logo (95%)
Mission statements (94%)	Statement of mission or philosophy (100%)
Details on how to donate money (91%)	Details on how to contribute money (82%)
Press releases (88%)	Press releases (60%)
Policy issue statements (81%)	Positions on policy issues (99%)
Updated information request function (68%)	Things that can be requested by e-mail or mail (96%)
Calendars of events (58%)	Calendars of events (76%)
Downloadable files or documents (48%)	Downloadable information (33%)
Speeches (28%)	Speeches (22%)
Downloadable graphic images (26%)	Downloadable graphics (18%)
Announcements of regularly scheduled news forums (10%)	Regularly scheduled news forums (21%)
Links to other nonprofit sites (8%)	Links to other Web sites (73%)
Online polls (3%)	Opportunity to vote on issues (44%)
Online surveys (2%)	Survey to voice opinion on issues (46%)
Statement inviting users to return (2%)	Statement inviting users to return (2%)

Relationships among adversarial organizations. Although building and maintaining an organization is a major goal of activists, their
primary goal is to "rectify the conditions" that they have agreed among
themselves are problematic (Smith & Ferguson, 2001, p. 294). Engaging
adversaries in policy discussions is often paramount to achieving such
goals. Issue-driven relationships include relationships formed from

Table 8.2   Content Analysis Items Reported by Kang and Norton (2004) but Not Taylor et al. (2001)

Kang and Norton's (2004) Characteristics of Largest U.S. Nonprofit Organizations' Web Sites
Contact information (100%)
Organizational history (96%)
Disclaimer or privacy policy (91%)
E-mail addresses (85%)
Size information about the organization (82%)
Community service information (81%)
Information about social responsibility (79%)
Annual reports (74%)
Links to local branches (59%)
Form to allow users to join organization online (57%)
Feedback forms (45%)
Discussion forums (8%)
Chat rooms (4%)

Table 8.3   Content Analysis Items Reported by Taylor et al. (2001) but Not Kang and Norton (2004)

Taylor et al.'s (2001) Occurrence of Dialogic Features on 100 Activist Web Sites
Identification of member base (81%)
Posting news stories in last 30 days (54%)
Links to political leaders (39%)
Frequently asked questions or question and answers (28%)

opposing sides as well as the relationships or alliances formed based on a common stance. Control mutuality is an especially important outcome to organizations that contest an issue initially as underdogs. As discussed in Chapter 5, control mutuality is "the degree to which the parties in a relationship are satisfied with the amount of control they have over a relationship" (Grunig, 2002, p. 2).

116   PUBLIC RELATIONS ONLINE

You will notice a sharp contrast between strategies designed to open conversations and strategies designed to shut them down. When opposing parties and their audiences see an issue as a legitimate topic of debate, heated discussion may ensue. For that debate to have any real meaning and to have any chance of turning into negotiation, both sides must acknowledge some balance of control in the conversation—control mutuality. Consider this September 6, 2005, entry on http://www.pizzadeliverydrivers.org/, the now defunct Web site for the Association of Pizza Delivery Drivers (APDD, 2005):

IPHFA [International Pizza Hut Franchise Association] & PHI [Pizza Hut International] now taking APDD seriously!
    After months of denying that APDD is a concern to them, and almost denying knowledge of APDD's existence, Pizza Hut International has made it's [sic] counsel (lawyer) for litigation and Human Resources, Erika Burkhardt, available to help franchisees. PHI encourages it's [sic] franchisees to be watchful for union activity by making sure operators are trained to recognize and respond to union activity.

The response to union activity turned out to include "union avoidance training," making it clear that the drivers still had a way to go in realizing mutual control in the relationship with Pizza Hut.

In more extreme cases of conflict, organizations may deem their detractors to be no more than online vandals. In these cases, public relations people are advised to work forcefully to chill the gears of the rumor mill. Take, for example, the advice of Parry Aftab (2005) to readers of the *Public Relations Strategist*. Aftab specializes in privacy cases in which organizations feel they have been flat-out attacked online, as opposed to engaged in meaningful dialogue. Far from shared control or relationship building as a response, Aftab calls for "cyberwarfare" in dealing with "cyberattacks":

Individuals (or competitor entities) may send hateful anonymous e-mails; launch IM, e-mail, text messaging, denial-of-service and spam campaign attacks; destroy or deface Web sites; or create Web sites that threaten companies and management. (p. 28).

In preparing for such warfare, Aftab (2005) recommends implementing policies to protect confidential information and to discourage rumors and harassment of company officials. She also recommends using electronic monitoring software and trained supervisors to review employee communications for policy violations. Penalties must be swift and strict, and a cyberbashing SWAT-team should be called in for follow-up.

Would you want to work at an organization with these policies in place? What do you think the relational outcomes of such strategies would be? Control mutuality? Trust? Satisfaction? Commitment? I doubt it—at least not without some serious discussion of the reasoning behind such measures. There is a thin line between freezing malicious misinformation and chilling productive dialogue. As she points out, "This is where good PR professionals can show their worth" (Aftab, 2005, p. 30).

❖ MAKING PEACE

Just as the Internet can be seen as a place for wars and battles, it also can be seen as a gathering place. Although it would be naïve to suggest that the Internet is some great elixir to social conflict, public relations people should be as ready to recognize its potential as an equalizer as they are to see it as a frightening place of cybercrime and cyberwarfare.

In 1988, Dean Kruckeberg and Kenneth Starck published a provoking book advocating the role of public relations in restoring and maintaining a sense of community in societies that they observed as increasingly fragmented. Although they recognized that more personalized communication technology was in some ways part of the problems of social fragmentation and anomie, they also pointed to the capacity of the same technologies to bring communities together. More than a decade later, Starck and Kruckeberg (2001) followed up on their work, taking into consideration trends in globalization and the rapid advance of online technologies in the 1990s. They remained optimistic: "Community building can be proactively encouraged and nurtured by corporations with the guidance and primary leadership of these organizations' public relations practitioners" (p. 59).

The potential for online public relations in issue-driven relationships lies with the practitioners. Although it will be necessary at times for practitioners to take defensive measures in protecting an organization's reputation (Aftab, 2005) and its digital assets (Hallahan, 2004), public relations people must work to balance protection and privacy with openness and transparency in online communication.

Professional advice and scholarship on relationship building in public relations gives us the nuts and bolts needed work toward such high ideals. The next chapter looks at how relational maintenance strategies like openness, positivity, task sharing, and networking can be translated into tips for building and maintaining online relationships.

118 PUBLIC RELATIONS ONLINE

❖ REFERENCES

Aftab, P. (2005). The PR professional's role in handling cyberwarfare. *Public Relations Strategist, 11*(3), 28–30.

Association of Pizza Delivery Drivers. (2005, September 6). *IPHFA & PHI now taking APDD seriously!* Available from http://www.pizzadeliverydrivers.org/

Barringer, F. (2005, July 18). Public relations campaign for research office at E.P.A. includes ghostwriting articles. *New York Times*, A1, 16. Available online at http://www.nytimes.com/2005/07/18/politics/18contracts.html?ex=1279339200&en=8f3a6ce62ef9bdc7&ei=5090&partner=rssuser land&emc=rss

Berners-Lee, T. (2005, October 10). *Web inventor: Online life will produce more creative children.* Retrieved June 14, 2006, from http://www.cnn.com/2005/TECH/internet/08/30/tim.berners.lee/

Coombs, W. T. (1998). The Internet as a potential equalizer: New leverage for confronting social irresponsibility. *Public Relations Review, 24*, 289–303.

Cutlip, S. M. (1994). *The unseen power: Public relations. A history.* Hillsdale, NJ: Erlbaum.

DiLorenzo, T. J. (1997). Life, liberty, and pizza delivery. *Freeman, 47*(5). Retrieved June 14, 2006, from http://www.libertyhaven.com/politicsand currentevents/crimeandterrorism/lifeliberty.shtml

Dougall, E., Fox, A., & Burton, L. J. (2001). Interactivity, influence and issues management: The impacts and implications of computer-mediated communication for Australian public relations practitioners. *Asia Pacific Public Relations Journal, 3*(2), 17–34.

Dutta-Bergman, M. J. (2005). Civil society and public relations: Not so civil after all. *Journal of Public Relations Research, 17*, 267–290.

Esrock, S. L., & Leichty, G. B. (1998). Social responsibility and corporate Web pages: Self-presentation or agenda-setting? *Public Relations Review, 24*, 305–319.

Grunig, J. E. (1997). A situational theory of publics: Conceptual history, recent challenges and new research. In D. Moss, T. MacManus, & D. Vercic (Eds.), *Public relations research: An international perspective* (pp. 3–48). Boston: International Thomson Business Press.

Grunig, J. E. (2002). *Qualitative methods for assessing relationships between organizations and publics.* Gainesville, FL: Institute for Public Relations. Retrieved June 14, 2006, from http://www.instituteforpr.com/relationships.phtml? article_id=2002_relationships_org_public

Grunig, J. E., & Hunt, T. (1984). *Managing public relations.* New York: Rinehart & Winston.

Hallahan, K. (2001). The dynamics of issues activation and response: An issues processes model. *Journal of Public Relations Research, 13*, 27–59.

Hallahan, K. (2004). Protecting an organization's digital public relations assets. *Public Relations Review, 30*, 255–268.

Heath, R. L. (1997). *Strategic issues management: Organizations and public policy challenges.* Thousand Oaks, CA: Sage.

Heath, R. L. (1998). New communication technologies: An issues management point of view. *Public Relations Review, 24,* 273–288.

Henderson, A. (2005). Activism in "paradise": Identity management in a public relations campaign against genetic engineering. *Public Relations Review, 17,* 117–138.

Kang, S., & Norton, H. E. (2004). Nonprofit organizations' use of the World Wide Web: Are they sufficiently fulfilling organizational goals? *Public Relations Review, 30,* 279–284.

Kruckeberg, D., & Starck, K. (1988). *Public relations and community: A reconstructed theory.* New York: Praeger.

Roper, J. (2002). Government, corporate, or social power? The Internet as a tool in the struggle for dominance in public policy. *Journal of Public Affairs, 2,* 113–124.

Smith, M. F., & Ferguson, D. P. (2001). Activism. In R. L. Heath (Ed.), *Handbook of public relations* (pp. 291–300). Thousand Oaks, CA: Sage.

Starck, K., & Kruckeberg, D. (2001). Public relations and community: A reconstructed theory revisited. In R. L. Heath (Ed.), *Handbook of public relations* (pp. 51–59). Thousand Oaks, CA: Sage.

Taylor, M., Kent, M. L., & White, W. J. (2001). How activist organizations are using the Internet to build relationships. *Public Relations Review, 27,* 263–284.

Zúniga, M. M. (2005, May 14). *ExxonMobil's echo chamber: Well-funded pseudoscience.* Retrieved June 14, 2006, from http://www.dailykos.com/story only/2005/5/14/185627/393

120   PUBLIC RELATIONS ONLINE

Hands-Online Activity

❖ TRUTH OR CONSEQUENCES

Find online news coverage of an issue that interests you. The story you find should meet three criteria: (1) be published or posted by a news organization you consider to be reputable, (2) be presented as a news story and not as an editorial or opinion piece, and (3) cite at least two named organizations that can be found online to discuss opposing sides of the issue.

1. Complete the following.
   a. Brief definition of the issue:

   b. Name of news organization:

   _____

   c. Name of organization/public on one side of issue:

   _____

   d. Name of organization/public on a different side of the same issue:

   _____

2. What are the controls on veracity of information for the online information provided by each of the three sources of information? That is, what are the consequences of not being truthful that keep these sources honest? (You might have to work on assumptions here.)

Issue-Driven Relationships   121

   a. News organization?

   b. Organization/Public 1?

   c. Organization/Public 2?

3. Choose one of the organizations/publics. If "rectifying the conditions" of the issue is a goal for that organization, and if that organization hired you to consult them on their online public relations efforts related to the issue, what would your main advice be?

4. In what ways can online media help the organization/public that you chose to side with to achieve its issue-based goals without the news media? Name at least two specific tactics.

9

Managing Public Relations in Real Time

Strategy, not technology, drives PR programs.

—John Guiniven (2005, p. 6)

❖ OVERVIEW

This chapter covers the interrelated roles of online planning, action, and communication in the cyclical process of strategic public relations. Online media serve as forums for public relations planning as well as tools for often high-speed organizational action and communication. This chapter will discuss issues to consider when public relations people work as members of geographically dispersed teams and online communities. Practical advice for online action and communication is offered based on interactive strategies for building and maintaining relationships.

124   PUBLIC RELATIONS ONLINE

❖ THE SPEED OF REAL TIME

In August 2000, a computer equipment company called Emulex unwittingly became the focus of a case study of the dark side of light-speed online communications. Early on a Friday morning in August 2000, an Emulex press release was posted on an Internet news distribution service called Internet Wire. (The service later became Market Wire.) The release said that Emulex's chief executive was resigning, that the U.S. Securities and Exchange Commission was investigating the company, and that its quarterly earnings report was being revised to show a loss instead of a profit. In just 16 minutes after the release was republished online by several major wire services, stock prices plunged from more than $103 per share to $43 per share (U.S. Securities and Exchange Commission, 2001). Misguided investors traded more than 2 million Emulex shares during that brief time. Other companies in similar businesses also noticed sell-offs as investors worried that the news from Emulex indicated sector-wide financial issues. But here's the catch—the news release was a hoax.

Emulex executives immediately notified the NASDAQ stock market that the news was phony, and NASDAQ officials temporarily halted trading of Emulex shares. Emulex CEO Paul Folino made multiple appearances on CNBC that day to ensure investors that he was still on the job and that the company had indeed turned profits in its quarterly earnings (Grice & Ard, 2000). Dow Jones, Bloomberg News, CBS Market-Watch, and TheStreet.com—all news services that had reported the false news—quickly followed with corrections. By 10:30 A.M. Pacific Time, Emulex shares were back on the market, and by the end of the day, they had recovered to a price of $105.75, but not before Emulex experienced the unwanted excitement of a $2.2-billion market capital thrill ride.

About the only part of this case that didn't move at digital speed was the follow-up investigation of Mark Jakob, a former Internet Wire employee who issued the phony release from a personal computer at El Camino College in Torrance, California. A year later, in 2001, he was sentenced to 44 months in prison after pleading guilty to charges of securities fraud and wire fraud.

Such is the speed of Internet buzz, which can hurt an organization as fast as it helps it. Can you do anything about it? Often you can, but it takes planning and interactive communication.

❖ PLANNING

Strategic public relations is all about the planning, action, and communication that result from ongoing research and evaluation efforts.

(Research and evaluation are covered in more detail in the next chapter.) The Emulex case shows just how fast an organization may need to respond to a situation in an online environment, and the better the strategic planning, the better prepared an organization is to adapt at the speed of online information. Real-time adaptation doesn't necessarily mean seat-of-the-pants public relations. Online media offer opportunities for strategic but interactive communication (i.e., contingency interactivity, in which each organization's and each public's action and communication depends on the action and communication of the other).

In the most practical sense, strategic public relations planning means developing goals and objectives. Goals are more general than objectives. Objectives specify measurable steps you take to achieve goals. Some situations, such as planning to overhaul an organization's Web site, might allow plenty of time to develop a very detailed strategy. A several-month timeline could be designed based on careful research, with a detailed budget and week-by-week objectives leading to a final product that accomplishes goals supporting the general mission of the organization. On the other hand, an unexpected emergency such as the Emulex case may require a quickly devised goal (e.g., recover market capital!) with on-the-spot objectives (e.g., notify NASDAQ now, get corrections out through all major wire services before noon). Even the latter case, however, can benefit from some degree of proactive planning.

Building a Web site. Let's first consider the planning that might go into building a Web site when planners have the luxury of working in an extended timeline. Then we can look at ways planning can help organizations respond to emerging issues in their environment as well as flat-out emergencies. General goals for Web sites may include keywords like *inform, sell*, and *persuade* (Diggs-Brown & Glou, 2004). And as we have seen in prior chapters, public relations goals for Web sites also might include more directed ideas such as generating publicity, responding to consumer concerns, and building coalitions. Writing realistic objectives to serve as steps to accomplishing these broader goals depends very much on your budget and timeline—key parts of the planning process in their own right. Budgets for building a Web site or any form of content management system should include the costs related to personnel (salaries, benefits, training, overhead) as well as the costs of technology and information (hardware, new or upgraded software, database subscriptions, etc.).

Internet publicity expert Steve O'Keefe (2002) suggests a three-part approach to getting an online publicity effort up and running. First, get the right software and get people familiar with using it. For building a Web site, this might include database software, HTML editors,

126 PUBLIC RELATIONS ONLINE

graphics programs, and FTP (file transfer protocol) applications. Second, "teach the documents," which means asking staff to work with various document formats such as spreadsheets, HTML, PDF, and Word (O'Keefe, 2002, p. 411). Document-based lessons include how to find documents online, how to format information for online presentation, how to address and send targeted e-mail messages, how to annotate bookmarks, and how to convert document content across formats. Testing is the final step O'Keefe recommends in planning to go live online. Testing is a good example of how evaluation can be done throughout an ongoing process of public relations and not just at the end of a campaign. Seeing how your Web page loads in different Web browsers, entering data from a remote terminal and seeing how that data feeds into your database, and sending automated response e-mails to your own inquiries are all examples of basic informal research that will help you work bugs out before going live with your Web page. This testing also illustrates the range of tasks that might require hiring or training team members as part of your plan.

Key skills in planning or overhauling a Web site include writing, graphic design, information architecture, database operations, and general system maintenance. For a simple Web page, you might be able to handle all this yourself with just a laptop, some Web editing software, and a server. But if you are designing a Web page to meet larger goals, you'll likely work with a number of different people bringing a variety of areas of expertise to the project.

Online teamwork. Working with different people handling different tasks to reach a common goal requires one of the most important public relations skills of all—management. Content management systems and wikis, as defined in Chapter 1, are a big part of getting the job done when you are working with people online.

Dan Forbush (2005), founder and president of ProfNet, which is a service of PR Newswire designed to make expert sources available to journalists, launched a wiki called www.katrinaexperts.com. The Hurricane Katrina-focused wiki offered constantly updated information from experts such as college and university professors to news media covering the disaster. Forbush suggests that, to be strategic, wikis used for public relations purposes need to be much more focused than all-inclusive content management systems (CMSs) like Wikipedia. He outlines four questions to ask as part of the planning process:

1. Who are the people you aim to enlist in this interaction?

2. What do you aim to achieve there?

3. What kind of content do you hope they'll be motivated to submit?

4. Who do you hope it will read it?

Meeting budget and timeline objectives means getting along with the people involved; with online projects, those people often work together in geographically dispersed teams (GDTs). Organizational networking consultants Jessica Lipnack and Jeffrey Stamps (2000) define a GDT as "a group of people who work interdependently with a shared purpose across space, time and organization boundaries using technology" (p. 18).

GDTs will work better in cases in which all members of the team are somewhat practiced with the constraints and issues that arise when working in online environments. Just getting acquainted with the cultural, geographical, and technological changes we face when we join such an effort is a big part of the job. Professor Gary Fontaine (2002) at the University of Hawai'i has conducted extensive research and training with GDTs and has found three key challenges:

1. Overcoming "ecoshock," which is a term Fontaine (2002) uses to describe our psychological reaction to strange new work environments. Symptoms include frustration, fatigue, clumsiness, rigid thinking, and anxiety.

2. Developing and implementing strategies to get things done. In culturally diverse teams, strategy options include adopting the ways of others, compromising, or coming up with new ways to do things altogether.

3. Maintaining motivation despite the lasting effects of ecoshock. Fontaine (2002) says this is the greatest challenge "because it takes time for ecoshock to diminish and for new strategies and skills to be developed and practised in order to get tasks done effectively" (p. 122).

In the example of building a Web site or an online publicity effort, we can see how planning can help increase your chances of accomplishing your tasks. For example, you'll want to provide opportunities for people to get acquainted as part of your timeline and budget. This is all based on the assumption that your goals and objectives are clear, as are the expectations of the members assigned to the team.

Online communities. Although a GDT may be considered a type of online community, the term *online community* generally connotes a larger group of people working together with less specifically defined

128   PUBLIC RELATIONS ONLINE

goals and less measurable objectives than a GDT working on developing a Web page for public relations purposes. Blogging communities are a good example. Sun Microsystems' blogs.sun.com is a good example of an online community using corporate blogs as a primary forum for communication. The site is described in a single sentence on its home page as a space "accessible to any Sun employee to write about anything" (Sun Microsystems, 2005). Microsoft also actively encourages employees to blog at blogs.msdn.com. Microsoft was the single largest host of corporate blogs in October 2004 according to data collected by Sifry (2004), who mused "that there is still a tremendous opportunity for forward-thinking companies and management to have a significant positive impact on their public perception" by way of hosting blogs.

Blogging policies of corporate blog pioneers show how some rules for managing these forms of communication were beginning to emerge in 2005. Fredrik Wackå (2005) compared the blog polices of eight of the most prominent corporate blog sites of June 2005, including IBM, Yahoo, and Sun, as well as public relations giant Hill & Knowlton. All eight included some variation of four core rules:

- Take personal responsibility for your blog posts
- Abide by the existing rules of your company
- Don't tell trade secrets
- Be nice and courteous

Hill & Knowlton's (2005) code of practice for its "Collective Conversation" blog is of particular interest to those working with (and within) online communities to achieve public relations goals and objectives. The stated goals of the Hill & Knowlton blogs are "to give our consultants the opportunity to participate in the blogosphere, to listen to and learn from our audiences, and to contribute their own vast insight and experience on topics related to our industry" (Hill & Knowlton, 2005). These goals are right in line with the concept of contingency interactivity, keeping the focus on the interaction of actual people using technologies to communicate.

Emergencies, crises, and disasters. Although thinking through the steps of a new Web site might allow plenty of time for planning and proactive management, and although developing guidelines for emerging online forums for communication might mean balancing reactions to new technologies with proactive goals and objectives, online crises such as the Emulex case offer the most extreme challenges to the concept of planning. This isn't to say that public relations people cannot do any planning for crises. Although there may be no way to plan for all the unpredictable effects of a large-scale disaster such as the September 11, 2001, attacks or Hurricane Katrina, online media can be used as part of a general disaster plan to allow for better communication when strategy must be developed on the spot.

At a very technical level, crisis plans can include computer security measures such as updated password systems; secure servers; firewalls; updated virus protection and anti-spyware programs; hardware backups; and satellite, dial-up, and battery-operated communication options if electrical systems go out (Silverman, 2005).

Middleberg (2001) recommends designing a contingency Web site that will be ready to activate in case your organization needs to make a quick shift from online business as usual to crisis management mode. Contingency sites should be ready to launch on very short notice and should include offline and online contact information for key executives and spaces where information can easily be posted and updated during the stress of a crisis.

Strategic planning, then, is not limited to predictable situations. Going live with a contingency Web site, writing guidelines for an emerging online community hosted by your organization, and responding to an online misinformation crisis are all ways that action and communication processes can flow from goals and objectives, which can be derived from past research and evaluation of issues and crises.

Questionable Claims

❖ INSTANT SYNERGY—JUST ADD TECHNOLOGY?

When students at the University of Hawai'i and Kansas State University worked in GDTs to produce strategic public relations plans, the students (and the professors) got a good example of the ups and downs of managing public relations work online. The students worked together using online bulletin boards and related educational technologies as very basic content management systems.

One assignment involved developing a strategic plan for promoting either genetically modified or organic papayas to Hawai'i residents aged 20 to 30. You might predict—as we did—that projects turned in by students working in teams consisting of both Kansas and Hawai'i students would demonstrate better understanding of the target public, the product category, and the range of relevant issues than projects turned in by comparable teams consisting of students in Kansas only. Yet independent judges rated the projects turned in by Hawai'i-Kansas teams to be no better than projects turned in by Kansas-only teams.

So what happened? At times, Hawai'i students wanted to know why Kansas students were in such a hurry, and Kansas students couldn't understand why Hawai'i students were missing deadlines. At times, the expectations were reversed. Sometimes the issues were cultural. Sometimes they were chronological. When it's 8:30 A.M. Tuesday in Manhattan, Kansas, it's 4:30 A.M. in Honolulu, unless you're on daylight savings time—then it's 3:30 A.M. in Honolulu. By 8 P.M. Honolulu time, it's Wednesday morning in Kansas. I'm now more wary than ever of the word *synergy*.

But the papaya projects did produce some fruit. We found that in all groups, the projects led to an increase of self-efficacy among students when it came to working with online media. It was a learning experience for all of us. So-called synergy isn't organic to online technology. It takes time and practice (O'Malley & Kelleher, 2002).

❖ ACTION AND COMMUNICATION PROCESSES

The relational strategies introduced in Chapter 5—positivity, openness, assurances, task sharing, social networks—can be used to build a rough outline for practical advice on online public relations.

Positivity. Keeping things positive in online public relations requires knowledge of how and why journalists, consumers, investors, activists, and other stakeholders go online in the first place. It also requires a good sense of netiquette that applies to working online with real people from any of these groups. One major value that public relations people offer clients is the quality (not just quantity) of human contacts in various stakeholder groups.

According to Virginia Shea (1994), who literally wrote the book on netiquette, Rule Number 1 is "Remember the human." For an example from the world of media relations, consider the advice of public relations counselor Ann Wylie (2004), who recommends writing less formally when contacting reporters via e-mail. She offers a quick self-test for readability of e-mail releases: "Say, 'Hey did you hear?' If the rest of your release sounds as if it could logically follow that level of informality, you're on the right track" (p. 14). You've got to re-write your press releases if you are going to send them as e-mail. Simply cutting the text and headings of a longer printed release and pasting them into an e-mail doesn't show much regard for the person on the other end.

Wylie (2004) also recommends keeping e-mail subject lines to less than five words, about the maximum most e-mail programs will show in the inbox, and working to fit your entire release on a single computer screen with contact information below to minimize the need for scrolling to get the scoop. This advice illustrates a cycle in the history of news media. The whole idea of writing news stories with the most important information in the lead (i.e., inverted pyramid style) has been attributed to telegraph technology that made editors fear losing the bottom part of a story if the transmission was interrupted (Scanlan, 2003). Always consider the person on the other end.

O'Keefe's (2002) point ("teach the documents") about how important it is to learn the ins and outs of various formats of online documents resonates here. Working well with online documents might mean simply reformatting and rewriting a news release for e-mail in media relations. But it also can mean learning to migrate annual report data to XBRL in financial relations (see Chapter 7) or taking a paper-based political letter to legislators and making it work online as a template for potential activists in issue-driven public relations efforts (see Chapter 8).

Openness. Perhaps the most common recommendation made in both public relations trade media and scholarly literature for online communications is this—post good contact information! If you are using e-mail, the Web, RSS, streaming media, or any other form of online communication to start a conversation, you must make sure you give receivers a reliable way to respond. Include your physical address, e-mail addresses, instant messaging information, telephone numbers, or any other way of contacting you that will actually work.

If you've got public information to share, put it in the digital sunshine. Financial documents such as annual and quarterly reports are the first thing that come to mind, but also consider posting white papers, speeches, and the like if you think these documents and audiovisual files might be useful in helping journalists, investors, consumers, and other stakeholders understand your organization and its leadership. Sharing an understandable flowchart with links to different parts of your organization also will help you make your organization's inner workings more transparent. And as discussed in Chapter 2, a well-designed organizational Web presence may work even better than a flowchart to help people see how your organization works.

Assurances. Remember the rhetorical importance of dialogue. The best way to assure publics that you are serious about online communication is to be responsive. Contact information is a good start, but make sure real people are available to answer inquiries at the points of contact you provide. Not having the human infrastructure to support a splendidly presented Web presence can undermine the whole effort. Barbara Long (2002), president of E-Savvy Communications, suggests that public relations people working with consumers online ask themselves, "Are you and your staff ready to respond to e-mails, answer questions, fill online orders, keep the site current and manage customer databases to generate e-mail coupons and newsletters?" (p. 23).

Assure your publics that any e-mail or other push communication they receive is totally optional. Only push materials if people opt in, and make it easy for them to opt out. In other words, assure them you're not a spammer.

Task sharing. Relationships flourish when people work to help each other out. This one comes directly from the research on interpersonal relationships (e.g., Stafford & Canary, 1991). Open-source efforts produce better results only when people take the time to improve a product such as a software program and then make that work publicly available. The same goes for news. Use online media to make yourself a generous source and your organization a generous resource to reporters.

Online media also are making it easier for public relations people to serve as better resources for each other. For example, online communication consultant Constantin Basturea (n.d.) started the NewPR Wiki (www.thenewpr.com/wiki) to offer the following:

- a repository of relevant information about how the PR practice is changing
- a collaboration tool for PR professionals and people interested in the practice of public relations
- an open space where anyone can ask questions, post ideas, or start a project.

Social networks. Systems theory works here. Remember that you don't work alone when you represent an organization. Rather, you work in a system that includes all the other people and departments in that organization. People might be interested in hearing from those others directly. Some public relations people are defensive about letting journalists and others talk to employees and members directly, and this apprehension is understandable because communicating with consistency, with "one voice," is such an important factor in integrated communication strategies, but it is probably unrealistic to expect to have total control over all points of online contact. So you're better off collaborating with both your colleagues and the news media to stay involved in the conversation. Talk with your colleagues about what they are talking about online. This is a more harmonious way to stay consistent in communications than trying to build firewalls and no-comment policies (Searls & Weinberger, 2001). This is easier said than done, but not impossible, especially in smaller companies.

Build your online action and communication efforts into external networks—the suprasystems in which you, your colleagues, and your publics work and play online. Linking to the work of other journalists, bloggers, and even competitors helps you put your actions and communication in context. Journalists doing research like to have context, as do activists seeking affiliations and consumers looking for marketplace conversations.

❖ REFERENCES

Basturea, C. (n.d.). *About.* Retrieved June 15, 2006, from http://www.the newpr.com/wiki/pmwiki.php?pagename=Main.About

Diggs-Brown, B., & Glou, J. L. G. (2004). *The PR styleguide: Formats for public relations practice.* Belmont, CA: Thomson/Wadsworth.

Fontaine, G. (2002). Teams in teleland: Working effectively in geographically dispersed teams "in" the Asia Pacific. *Team Performance Management, 8,* 122–133.

Forbush, D. (2005, September 20). *When creating a wiki, know your purpose.* Paper presented at the Global PR Blogweek 2.0 conference. Retrieved June 15, 2006, from http://www.globalprblogweek.com/2005/09/20/forbush-wiki-focused-purpose/

Grice, C., & Ard, S. (2000, August 25). *Hoax briefly shaves $2.5 billion off Emulex's market cap.* Retrieved June 15, 2006, from http://news.com.com/2100-1033-244975.html

Guiniven, J. (2005, September). Podcast as PR tool: What do you need to know? *Public Relations Tactics, 12*(9), 6.

Hill & Knowlton. (2005). Collective Insight is Hill & Knowlton's blogging community. Retrieved November 4, 2005, from http://blogs.hilland knowlton.com/blogs/about.aspx

Lipnack, J., & Stamps, J. (2000). *Virtual teams: People working across boundaries with technology.* New York: John Wiley & Sons.

Long, B. S. (2002, November). How to avoid common Web mistakes. *Public Relations Tactics, 9*(11), 23.

Middleberg, D. (2001). *Winning PR in the wired world: Powerful communications strategies for the noisy digital space.* New York: McGraw-Hill.

O'Keefe, S. (2002). *Complete guide to Internet publicity: Creating and launching successful online campaigns.* New York: John Wiley & Sons.

134   PUBLIC RELATIONS ONLINE

O'Malley, M., & Kelleher, T. (2002). Papayas and pedagogy: Geographically dispersed teams and Internet self-efficacy. *Public Relations Review, 28,* 175–184.

PR Innovation of the Year 2006. (2006). Retrieved June 15, 2006, from http://www.prweek.com/us/events/index.cfm?fuseaction=awardDetail &id=23769

Scanlan, C. (2003, Dec. 17). *Writing from the top down: Pros and cons of the inverted pyramid.* Retrieved June 15, 2006, from http://www.poynter.org/column.asp?id=52&aid=38693

Searls, D., & Weinberger, D. (2001). Markets are conversations. In R. Levine, C. Locke, D. Searls, & D. Weinberger (Eds.), *The cluetrain manifesto: The end of business as usual* (pp. 75–114). New York: Perseus.

Shea, V. (1994). *Netiquette.* San Rafael, CA: Albion. Retrieved June 15, 2006, from http://www.albion.com/netiquette/book/index.html

Sifry, D. (2004, October 17). *Oct 2004 state of the blogosphere: Corporate bloggers.* Retrieved June 15, 2006, from http://www.sifry.com/alerts/archives/000390.html

Silverman, B. (2005). *PR fuel: Preparing for a disaster.* Retrieved June 15, 2006, from http://www.ereleases.com/pr/preparing_disaster.html

Stafford, D. J., & Canary, L. (1991). Maintenance strategies and romantic relationship type, gender and relational characteristics. *Journal of Social and Personal Relationships, 8,* 217–242.

Sun Microsystems. (2005). *Blogs.sun.com.* Retrieved June 15, 2006, from http://blogs.sun.com

U.S. Securities and Exchange Commission. (2001, August 8). *Defendant in Emulex hoax sentenced* (Litigation Release No. 17094). Retrieved June 15, 2006, from http://www.sec.gov/litigation/litreleases/lr17094.htm

Wacká, F. (2005, June 6). Policies compared: Today's corporate blogging rules. Retrieved June 15, 2006, from http://www.corporateblogging.info/2005/06/policies-compared-todays-corporate.asp

Wylie, A. (2004, August). Reach reporters with e-mail news releases. *Public Relations Tactics, 11*(8), 14.

Managing Public Relations in Real Time   135

Hands-Online Activity

❖ BLOGS AND STRATEGY

Hass MS&L, a firm that specializes in auto industry public relations, won *PR Week's* 2006 "Innovation of the Year" award for working with General Motors (GM) to launch the GM Fastlane blog (http://fast lane.gmblogs.com/). The blog site served as a channel for top-level GM executives (namely, GM Vice-Chairman Bob Lutz) to make daily entries during the 2005 Detroit Auto Show and continues beyond that as an ongoing forum. The GM blog also allows Internet users to post comments, to which GM executives regularly respond. According to *PR Week*:

> While some corporations were already operating blogs, GM was one of the first Fortune 500 companies to have such a successful one, in a year in which it desperately wanted to woo back customers and reestablish itself as an innovative company. ("PR Innovation of the Year," 2006)

One of the measurable objectives toward these broader goals was to attract 1,000 visitors a day during the blog's first months online. GM also sought links from marketing, public relations, and car enthusiast blogs. The blog got more than 1.3 million hits in its first nine months. The blog planners also calculated that 90% of media impressions were positive.

1. Do the huge number of hits and positive media impressions indicate success for GM in the broader goals of wooing customers and positioning itself as an innovator? If so, how? If no, why not?

2. Find another example of a corporate blog, as defined in Chapter 1.

136   PUBLIC RELATIONS ONLINE

Name or URL of corporate blog site:

_____

3. What do you think the goals of this blog site are? (If you can find the goals stated explicitly, that's even better.)

4. In the final chapter, we will look at how public relations people use online media to evaluate their efforts. If objectives are measurable steps taken toward goals, how might the outcomes of the blog you named in Number 2 be measured? Answer by writing at least two measurable objectives that public relations people could use to determine whether the broader goals for the blog are being met.

Objective 1:

Objective 2:

10

Applied Research and Evaluation

My aim is to orient you sufficiently for you to ask for help effectively.

—Earl Babbie, introducing a text section called "Social Research in Cyberspace" (1998, p. A10)

❖ OVERVIEW

Aside from tying the ends together in the loop of responsive, cyclical public relations, research and evaluation serve practitioners well to demonstrate what their bosses and clients are getting for their money. This chapter introduces the online offshoots of public relations research methods including surveys, experiments, interviews, focus groups, and content analyses. Usability and methods for tracking online communication also are discussed as ways of seeing that online public relations efforts are effectively interactive.

138   PUBLIC RELATIONS ONLINE

❖ THE VALUE IN EVALUATION

Some methods for determining the value (i.e., evaluating) of online communication efforts are online extensions of traditional research methods. These include surveys, experiments, interviews, focus groups, and content analyses. Other methods, particularly those that focus on types of human-computer interaction, are particularly appropriate for computer-mediated communication. Usability testing is a prime example. These are all *primary research methods* because they require that you go out and set up your own studies to collect your own information. Remember, however, that the Internet has drastically increased our access to data from research that has already been done.

When you work from data that someone else has collected and analyzed, this is *secondary research*, and in many cases, secondary research can be very informative and cost-effective. Census data, online scholarly journals, trade organization data, knowledge blogs, public opinion polls, library holdings, and even case studies of prior public relations efforts are all available online.

We talk a big game about research in public relations classes at colleges and universities. We make students do it over and over again. But why? And why is it worth covering yet again in a text on online public relations?

Lynne Sallot and Lance Porter conducted a series of studies on how U.S. public relations practitioners were using the Web and how they thought their own Web use influenced their power in their organizations (Porter & Sallot, 2005; Sallot, Porter, & Acosta-Alzura, 2004). They found that Web access was helping practitioners—even solo practitioners and those working in small organizations—to "easily conduct sophisticated evaluation," and that the Web offered "a tangible way to measure results" (Sallot et al., 2004, p. 274).

When Porter and Sallot (2005) asked more than 400 public relations people how often they used the Web for an array of 17 tasks ranging from improving pitches to managing issues, they found that the following five uses of the Web loaded onto a single factor (i.e., clumped together in the statistical results): (1) tracking press release usage, (2) doing research, (3) evaluating public relations work, (4) monitoring the competition, and (5) subscribing to customizable news alerts (p. 115). Moreover, Porter and Sallot found that those who scored higher on this research-and-evaluation factor were more likely to attribute their success in getting promoted to their Web use. The research-and-evaluation factor also was a key component of a practitioner profile that Porter and Sallot called a "super user." Super users of online media credit much of their achievement, as well as their expertise and prestige in organizations, to Web use.

Besides power and prestige, two often-cited reasons for adopting online research techniques are speed and economy (Johnson, 1997; Springston, 2001). Surveys, for example, can be distributed online much faster than they can be mailed, and there is no extra cost for postage. Keyword searches of online articles are much easier than scanning the pages of newspapers and magazines the old-fashioned way. And getting a group of people from several different continents to discuss your latest campaign in an online forum can be a lot cheaper than buying everyone plane tickets. But every method of research available online also has some drawbacks. Let's consider the pros and cons of some specific examples of primary research in online public relations.

❖ SURVEYS

Writing and design. Those little check boxes and radio buttons are so easy to make on a Web page, it's no wonder the Web is full of surveys and response forms. And commercial Web survey services have made it even easier to design surveys for online data collection and analysis. As with any research, though, designing a useful online survey means asking the right questions. This is largely a matter of strategy—what do you need to know from your publics to help you make informed decisions about your public relations efforts? Once you've determined your general research questions, you will need to convert those questions into relatively simple and understandable survey items. This is where public relations practitioners are forced to start thinking about their survey research from the perspective of the people responding rather than the people who want the answers to the questions. Are the questions easy to follow? Are there too many of them? How far do respondents have to scroll down each page of the survey, and how long will the whole survey take? What would motivate someone to spend the time and effort needed to complete the survey anyway? Writing a good online survey requires thinking through all these questions as well as the questions you're out to get answered by online publics. Yet writing and designing surveys is only part of the process of survey research.

Sampling and response rates. Finding the right people to complete surveys is a big challenge, whether you are doing your surveys online or not. One advantage of online sampling is that researchers can reach publics who otherwise would be very hard to find, at least in self-organized groups (Wright, 2005). Weather fanatics, Volkswagen

140   PUBLIC RELATIONS ONLINE

drivers, auction enthusiasts, religious youth groups, poker players—you name the topic and chances are you will be able to find some group of interested people online. But just because you find them doesn't mean you have a statistically representative sample of the larger population to work with. For example, people involved in the discussions on www.vwworld.com all may have some interest in discussing Volkswagens, but they don't necessarily represent the whole universe of Volkswagen drivers. Again, the researcher must go back to his research questions to determine whether the actual population—let's say "people who have posted a question or response on the www.vwworld.com Web site in the past six months"—is the group he wants to hear from. If this more narrowly defined population is indeed one of interest to the researcher, then he faces two more issues: How many of these people would be willing to respond to the survey (some in the group might even find a survey request to be spam-like and offensive), and how can he get in touch with them?

If e-mail addresses are available, the e-mail list might provide a sampling frame. The researcher then could send a plea to the list for people to go to a specific URL and complete a survey. Even then, however, those who choose to respond probably won't accurately represent the whole group of people with valid e-mail addresses. Most probably will ignore the request. Some may reply with bogus responses. Some may respond multiple times just to be funny. Response tracking software can help with the last concern by requiring people to provide an ID number or e-mail address, but this might deter some people from responding at all.

Assuming the researcher is willing to accept some compromises in developing a suitable sampling frame for his survey, the next challenge is getting enough people to respond to make the aggregate data meaningful. By adapting ideas that have worked for paper and telephone surveys, and by trial and error, online researchers have come up with some tips for increasing response rates (Gaddis, 2001; Jensen & Bhaskaran, n.d.; Wright, 2005):

- Personalize invitations to participate
- Tell people how you found them and why you're contacting them
- Be up front about who you are and what you are trying to accomplish
- Think through the costs and benefits (to respondents as well as to you and your organization) and explain them concisely
- Respect and protect respondents' identities with clearly explained procedures for handling their personal information

Applied Research and Evaluation   141

- Offer incentives such as coupons or entry into prize drawings
- Offer to share the results of your study
- Let people ask you questions, and answer them promptly
- Appeal to people's interests in expressing their own opinions
- Send polite follow-up requests to those who haven't responded (but if possible, try not to bother those who have responded— response tracking software can help here)
- Don't bother those who have given any indication they don't want to participate (this includes implicit and explicit rules for online forums)
- Make your survey user friendly
- Give people a deadline, just don't make it too soon

❖ EXPERIMENTS

Survey instruments can be applied as part of experimental design. As with scientific survey research, the careful design of valid experiments requires some knowledge of statistics and research methods. But the general logic of experimental design can be applied with varying degrees of validity, ranging from casual pseudo-experiments to very scientific studies. A key concept in any experimental design is control. The more control a researcher has over the conditions she is observing, the clearer her understanding will be of which independent variables are affecting which dependent variables. That is, she can make a better cause-effect argument to show the value of her work.

By controlling the conditions that survey respondents experience, you can turn survey research into experimental research. In a very simple scenario, you could design two different Web pages, then randomly direct users who go to your organization's home page to just one of the two pages. You would ask users to review the page and complete a survey. Offering an incentive like a gift certificate or entry into a prize drawing would increase your chances of getting enough people from both conditions to fill out the survey.

The random assignment to one group or the other is so that you can realistically expect that any differences in responses between the two groups probably are not related to outside variables. If your assignment process is truly random, then Volkswagen enthusiasts, salsa fans, pinochle players, waveriders, and retirees are just as likely to end up in one group as the other. That way you don't expect one group to respond in a certain way because its members included more surfers or retired people or some other category you're not interested

142   PUBLIC RELATIONS ONLINE

in measuring. If the groups are big enough (any less than 12 in each group and you will likely have some statistical problems), and the assignments are truly random, then the only real differences you would expect between groups would be caused by the differences in the Web pages they reviewed. Because you control that part, you are in a good position to observe cause-effect relationships. If the survey results show that one group trusts the organization more, found online information faster, or is more likely to make a donation, then you just might have some proof that the Web page that group reviewed is a better public relations tool for your purposes than the Web page the other group reviewed. Statistics could be applied to determine the significance of that difference.

Of course, expert experimental design means making a whole bunch of careful decisions: sampling and group assignments, question wording, design of conditions, and statistical analyses to name a few. But the payoff is being able to make a more compelling case that public relations outcomes (e.g., trust, news story interest, donations, volunteers, etc.) are caused by public relations tactics (e.g., a newly designed Web page, an online town hall forum, podcasting service, etc.).

❖ INTERVIEWS AND FOCUS GROUPS

Although surveys and experiments yield numbers and statistics (i.e., quantitative data), interviews and focus groups give researchers more qualitative information to work with. Qualitative methods allow participants to discuss issues in terms more true to their own experiences. In a direct interview, the researcher asks a respondent some carefully thought-out questions then lets the respondent elaborate on her answers. The researcher follows up with probes and other questions as appropriate, being careful not to lead the interviewee to unauthentic answers and discussion.

Focus groups involve a similar balance between the researcher's interests and the respondents' own thoughts and words. Focus groups are basically small-group interviews. Online interviews and focus groups can work for public relations practitioners who are looking to brainstorm ideas, tap the thinking of key publics, or evaluate new products, promotions, and campaigns (Gaddis, 2001).

Taking traditionally face-to-face techniques such as interviews and focus groups online may offer some of the same benefits as more quantitative methods, namely, speed and economy. Naturally, you will face some limitations as well. Here are some issues to consider when conducting or analyzing interviews and focus groups via e-mail, chats, and discussion forums.

Time. Perhaps the most important time-related issue in online communication is the distinction between asynchronous and real-time discussion. Real-time discussion happens faster, making it quicker in terms of collecting data. But the usefulness of those data in text-based real-time communication may be limited by the fact that people often can't type as fast as they think and talk. This is even more of a problem in group communication—by the time one person finishes typing a response to a topic, another already may have posted a question or comment taking the discussion in a whole different direction. Although the transcripts of such real-time discussions can be archived and analyzed later, the actual text may be fragmented and limited in the amount of careful thought it reveals. But online media do allow people to conduct voice- and video-based real-time conferencing, which are closer to the "real thing" of conducting face-to-face interviews or focus groups. These technologies are getting cheaper and more accessible.

Asynchronous communications have the advantage of letting people think through their responses before sending them. Of course, this takes more time for both the researcher and the respondents, but the outcomes may be worth it. One-to-one interviews can be conducted by e-mail. Online focus groups can be held in researcher-moderated forums, which could be password protected if the topics of discussion are sensitive and candid responses are a primary concern. Asynchronous communications also make it possible to collect responses across time (i.e., longitudinally). Reactions to a pilot public relations campaign, for example, might change as the campaign progresses, and a series of discussions over time can reveal those changes.

Space. Online qualitative researchers Nikihilesh Dholakia and Dong Zhang (2004) make a distinction between research spaces that are researcher defined and those that are subject defined (as well as those that are mutually defined). Researcher-defined spaces are hosted by the researcher. A special discussion forum set up on a company intranet is an example. Participants (or "interviewees" or "subjects") can then go to that online space to take part in the study. Subject-defined spaces include existing bulletin board systems, chat rooms, or blogs in which the researcher joins a discussion that already may be in progress. Although these forums might at first be attractive as ready-made places to get a study going, dropping in uninvited poses some netiquette issues. The researcher must be especially careful not to make himself unwelcome by trying too hard to control the direction of a conversation. He also must be careful not to deceive participants regarding his identity or intents.

144   PUBLIC RELATIONS ONLINE

Anonymity. Although a researcher should not deceive interviewees and focus group participants about his own identity, he might find it worthwhile to allow respondents to remain anonymous. The idea is that people might be more forthcoming and candid if they are not worried about their identities or possible repercussions from an employer or social group. In conducting interviews with employees about management practices, for example, researchers likely will get more candid responses if employees aren't worried about their bosses' reactions to them personally.

Bias. As discussed in the section on survey research, sampling bias can be a limitation in interpreting how well information gathered from a specific group of people online represents larger populations. Because qualitative research very often is conducted with smaller groups of people selected for specific criteria, the researcher's goal usually isn't to form a sample that statistically represents some large population. So sampling bias is usually expected—maybe even built in—in focus groups and interviews. A researcher might want to talk to disgruntled bloggers specifically because they *are* disgruntled bloggers, not because they represent some larger population of global Internet users.

Interviewer bias, on the other hand, is normally a much greater concern in qualitative research. To what degree does an interviewer influence the responses of participants? In both online and face-to-face contexts, careful wording can help an interviewer avoid "leading" interviewees too much. But avoiding nonverbal cues is easier in online interviews. Nonverbal cues include the wide eyes, reassuring smiles, crossed arms, subtle nods, puzzled brows, and so forth that suggest to respondents whether they are on the "right track" with their answers. With online media, an interviewer can stick to careful wording and avoid sending extra signals (Gaddis, 2001). So an interviewee's responses may be less likely to represent a larger population, but at least those responses in qualitative studies will be more likely to represent their own thinking and feelings rather than the interviewer's thoughts and ideas.

Participation. Although walking the line between drawing meaningful ideas from participants and over-influencing their responses can be tricky, so too can be getting participants to participate at all in a group context. Even once people are on board for a focus group, they may choose to remain relatively silent, especially in groups in which some people just tend to say more than others. Gaddis (2001) suggests that online focus groups can be moderated in such a way as to level out the responses. The tendency for some individuals to drown out the contributions of others may be "lessened by the fact that each respondent answers the moderator's question simultaneously behind the 'safety' of a screen name" (Solomon, 1996, p. 10).

Another benefit of online media for participation is the convenience of getting people from all over the globe, or maybe just all over the office, to participate at times and places that are convenient to them.

❖ USABILITY

Although the rapid rise of the Internet has given public relations practitioners new opportunities to show their value by offering tools for research and evaluation, at the same time, it has encouraged haste among professional communicators caught up in "an unbridled rush" to make a presence online (Hallahan, 2001, p. 223). Usability research offers an antidote to cases of hasty–Web site syndrome, which includes symptoms such as bad link structures, confusing layout, and inadvertently hidden information. Web design consultant Jakob Nielsen (2003), whose name is more commonly associated with the concept of Web site usability than any other, defines *usability* as "a quality attribute that assesses how easy user interfaces are to use" as well as "methods for improving ease-of-use during the design process." What makes usability so important in public relations is how it gets practitioners to take into account the way publics experience mediated communication with organizations.

Three key steps are essential to the process of usability testing: (1) getting a sample of users, (2) asking them to perform tasks that represent the things you hope others like them will be able to do, and (3) observing them as they try to do these tasks. The same sampling issues discussed previously apply here—you'll want your test users to represent a larger population, but you will also probably need to accept some compromises to work with a manageable number of people (Nielsen, 2003, recommends at least five) who are willing to participate without requiring budget-breaking bribes. The second two steps are what really separate user testing from the other research methods discussed thus far. Watching and listening to people as they work with your Web page or other online interfaces is different than having them fill out a survey or discuss the process in an interview. In examining usability, "Listening to what people say is misleading: you have to watch what they actually do" (Nielsen, 2003).

❖ UNOBTRUSIVE METHODS

The range of research options discussed so far goes from primarily quantitative methods (e.g., large-sample surveys with numerically

146   PUBLIC RELATIONS ONLINE

analyzed results) to much more qualitative methods (e.g., direct observations or analyses of longer written responses in asynchronous online interviews). What all these methods have in common is that they let you hear directly from the people you are most interested in. Direct responses are usually a good thing in communication research, but as we've seen, getting direct responses sometimes means bothering people who are important to you, which usually isn't very high on your list of public relations goals. At times, it might make better sense to use less-obtrusive measures.

Server data. Practitioners can look at server log files to identify the general locations and patterns of use of people and computers that access an organization's online resources. Server log analyzers are software programs that make it easier to make sense of the data, showing the number of "click-thrus" from one page to others and information identifying the search engines and referring pages that lead visitors to your Web site.

Online clipping and tracking services. These services offer public relations people the chance to see where in the online world their names and issues are popping up. Although the numbers are important in tracking mentions, more qualitative aspects of real-time and archived online fodder perhaps are even more valuable. "We look at the blogosphere as a focus group with 15 million people going on 24/7," Rick Murray, executive vice president of Edelman public relations told the *Wall Street Journal* (as cited in Bulkeley, 2005). The *Wall Street Journal* article discussed how public relations practitioners and brand managers are using automated blog-tracking services with features such as "natural-language processing" and "unstructured data mining" to speed up a process that otherwise would take near forever—culling through all the blog content on a particular topic.

Although such fee-based, content-analyzing, blog-tracking services reached six-digit annual costs for large accounts in 2005, some services with fewer features remain very inexpensive if not free. Among the major options are Technorati, "a real-time search engine that keeps track of what is going on in the blogosphere" and the Yahoo! buzz index, which offers a "buzz score" by computing "the percentage of Yahoo! users searching for that subject on a given day, multiplied by a constant to make the number easier to read" ("About Technorati," n.d.; "Yahoo! Buzz Index Help," n.d.). Straight quantitative services such as keyword counts are generally cheaper than services that offer more sophisticated quantitative and qualitative analyses.

Content analysis. Content analysis is "a systematic reading of a body of texts, images, and symbolic matter" (Krippendorff, 2003, p. 3). Just as surveys, experiments, focus groups, and interviews all have their online offshoots, so too does content analysis. And just as the other methods range from do-it-yourself techniques to high-end, high-powered scientific analysis, content analysis varies across the spectrum from casual and barely valid to statistically sound.

Being systematic is key in getting worthwhile results that aren't overly biased. The typical process includes the following steps. First a researcher must carefully identify what she is looking for (i.e., her research question). What are bloggers saying about our new Google ads? How are other environmental groups portraying our organization online? The second step is sampling. Instead of getting a sample of people though, the researcher works to find a sample of media content; ideally, the sample will represent a larger population of content. Computer analyses also allow online researchers to look at whole populations as well as samples. For example, a researcher might be able to find every single mention of her organization's URL in a particular online forum. The next step is to think through the procedures for coding data. In analyzing media coverage of an organization or product, a very simple coding scheme might include categories of "positive," "negative," and "neutral." Getting multiple people to look at the data is important here to make sure that there is some agreement on what constitutes a "positive," "negative," or "neutral" comment. The people who do look at the data are trained as coders. The idea is to avoid bias in coding. The number of times that multiple coders look at the same data and agree on the categories yields a statistic called intercoder (or interrater) reliability. Then, once all the data have been coded, the researcher can get into the actual analysis stage. The process includes characteristics of both quantitative and qualitative research.

Social network analysis. Online social network analysis seems especially appropriate for public relations (Paine & Lark, 2005). Whereas typical units of analysis in social research are individual people and their characteristics such as demographics, knowledge, attitudes, and behavior, as well as the contents of their communication, research on publics and organizations often calls for analysis of groups and the relations in and among the group members. Major online social networks include Friendster, MySpace, and Facebook. As online researcher Caroline Haythornthwaite (n.d.) puts it, "To understand how people work together, form communities, or gain access to information, it is necessary to examine the types of interactions they engage in."

148   PUBLIC RELATIONS ONLINE

❖ WHAT TO EVALUATE

Although wikis and Web forums, pressrooms and podcasts, and e-mail and extranets can be seen as the outputs of online public relations, the real products of social research and usability tests are people's perceptions of and experiences with these communication tactics. Perceptions and experiences, and the changes in people's knowledge, attitudes, and behaviors that go along with them, are better thought of as *outcomes* of online public relations. Of course, relationships are essential outcomes of online public relations, and one indicator of the quality of those relationships may be the quality of the contents of online conversations. Haythornthwaite's (n.d.) approach to studying social network relations reminds us of one underlying concept that, like the process of communication itself, can be seen as both the output and the outcome of online public relations. That underlying idea—a lasting concept—is interactivity.

There's a buzzword that techies use—"Web 2.0." It refers to the interactive, dynamic, user-generated, socially networked world of wikis, MySpace, bloggers, personal syndication, and peer-to-peer resource sharing. This is a different place than the more static Web we knew in the late 1990s. Its participatory, conversational style is right in line with public relations theory and research (i.e., relational approaches, contingency theory, etc.). But making sense of the dynamic processes that characterize this fluid network of networks and finding metrics for the outcomes are some of the most important challenges for online public relations. Then we'll be on to Web 3.0—whatever that will look like!

❖ REFERENCES

About Technorati. (n.d.). Retrieved June 16, 2006, from http://www.technorati.com/about/

Babbie, E. (1998). *The practice of social research* (8th ed.). Belmont, CA: Wadsworth.

Bulkeley, W. M. (2005, June 23). Marketers scan blogs for brand insights. *Wall Street Journal,* p. B1.

Dholakia, N., & Zhang, D. (2004, May). Online qualitative research in the age of e-commerce: Data sources and approaches. *Forum Qualitative Sozialforschung/Forum: Qualitative Social Research, 5*(2). Retrieved June 16, 2006, from http://www.qualitative-research.net/fqs-texte/2-04/2-04dholakiazhang-e.htm

Gaddis, S. E. (2001). On-line research techniques for the public relations practitioner. In R. L. Heath (Ed.), *Handbook of public relations* (pp. 591–602). Thousand Oaks, CA: Sage.

Hallahan, K. (2001). Improving public relations Web sites through usability research. *Public Relations Review, 27,* 223–239.

Haythornthwaite, C. (n.d.). *Caroline Haythornthwaite: My research interests.* Retrieved June 16, 2006, from http://people.lis.uiuc.edu/~haythorn/research_cah.html

Jensen, J. M., & Bhaskaran, V. (n.d.). *Ten easy ways to increase response rates for your online survey.* Retrieved June 16, 2006, from http://www.questionpro.com/akira/showArticle.do?articleID=deploy01

Johnson, M. A. (1997). Public relations and technology: Practitioner perspectives. *Journal of Public Relations Research, 9,* 213–236.

Krippendorff, K. (2003) *Content analysis: An introduction to its methodology* (2nd ed.). Thousand Oaks, CA: Sage.

Nielsen, J. (2003, August 25). *Usability 101: An introduction to usability.* Retrieved June 16, 2006, from http://www.useit.com/alertbox/20030825.html

Paine, K. D., & Lark, A. (2005, March). *How to measure blogs and other consumer generated media and what to do with the data once you have it.* Paper presented at the 8th International Public Relations Research Conference, Miami, FL. Retrieved June 16, 2006, from http://www.instituteforpr.com/pdf/K_Paine_A_Lark_March_2005.pdf

Porter, L. V., & Sallot, L. M. (2005). Web power: A survey of practitioners' World Wide Web use and their perceptions of its effects on their decision-making power. *Public Relations Review, 31,* 111–119.

Sallot, L. M., Porter, L. V., & Acosta-Alzura, C. (2004). Practitioners' Web use and perceptions of their own roles and power: A qualitative study. *Public Relations Review, 30,* 269–278.

Solomon, M. B. (1996). Targeting trendsetters. *Marketing Research: A Magazine of Management & Applications, 8,* 9–11.

Springston, J. K. (2001). Public relations and new media technology: The impact of the Internet. In R. L. Heath (Ed.), *Handbook of public relations* (pp. 603–614). Thousand Oaks, CA: Sage.

Wright, K. B. (2005). Researching Internet-based populations: Advantages and disadvantages of online survey research, online questionnaire authoring software packages, and Web survey services. *Journal of Computer-Mediated Communication, 10*(3), Article 11. Retrieved June 16, 2006, from http://jcmc.indiana.edu/vol10/issue3/wright.html

Yahoo! Buzz index help. (n.d.). Retrieved June 16, 2006, from http://help.yahoo.com/help/us/buzz/

150   PUBLIC RELATIONS ONLINE

Hands-Online Activity

❖ ONLINE RESEARCH

Choose a public relations program or campaign to consider for this exercise. Here are some options you might work with:

- public relations project that you are working on in school
- public relations campaign or program that you are working on in your job or volunteer work (or that you would like to start soon)
- hypothetical campaign to support one side of the issue that you identified in the Chapter 8 Hands-Online Activity

1. Peruse studies, reports, and data that are available online that might be relevant to your program or campaign. Some collections to get you started:

   a. Pew Internet & American Life Project—A "non-profit research center studying the social effects of the Internet on Americans" (see http://www.pewinternet.org/).

   b. *The Journal of Computer-Mediated Communication*—"A web-based, peer-reviewed scholarly journal. Its focus is social science research on computer-mediated communication via the Internet, the World Wide Web, and wireless technologies" (see http://jcmc.indiana.edu/).

   c. Eurobarometer—"The website for the Public Opinion Analysis sector of the European Commission" (see http://europa.eu.int/comm/public_opinion/).

   d. Asiabarometer—"The largest ever, comparative survey in Asia, covering East, Southeast, South and Central Asia" (see http://avatoli.ioc.u-tokyo.ac.jp/~asiabarometer/).

2. Identify one specific study, report, or data set that you might use to inform your project. This is secondary research. Name and reference (or URL):

Applied Research and Evaluation   151

3. Discuss the specific ways that you can use this research in your project. (What does it tell you that will help you develop a strategy? Does it suggest ways that you can measure the outcomes of your work? Or does it offer data that you can use for comparison with your specific project and publics?)

4. Most secondary research is limited in how specifically it can be used in public relations programs and campaigns. This is why primary research is so important.

   a. Name one specific research question or hypothesis you might put forward *after* reviewing the secondary research.

   b. What method of primary research would you look into first to answer this question or hypothesis? Is online research an option for that method? Is it the best option? Explain your answers.

Index

Action and communication step,
    of public relations, 23
Active publics, 112–113
Activist organizations, 113
Adversarial organizations, 114–117
Aggregators, 8
Alerts, 80
Alliances, 113
Assurances, 67–68, 131–132
Asymmetrical public relations, 45–46
Asynchronous communications,
    5–6, 143
Audio, streaming, 39–40

Beat diversity, 84–85
Bias, 144, 147
Blogs
   definition of, 7
   example of, 64
   organizational hosting of, 66
   tracking services for, 146
Boundaries, 17
Boundary spanning, 20–21
Brochureware, 37–39
Business to business, 90
Business to consumer, 90

Cause-effect relationships, 142
   CGM. See Consumer-generated
     media
   Chats, 5–6
   Clipping and tracking
     services, 146

Closed systems
   definition of, 18
   reactive strategies of, 23
Commerce-driven relationships
   consumers, 97–99
   customers, 97–99
   donors, 99
   frequently asked questions,
     91–92
   general-access facts, 91–92
   investors, 99
   overview of, 89–90
   technology, 90–95
   Web pages, 90–91
Commitment, 69
Communal relationship, 69–70
Communication
   asynchronous, 5–6, 143
   circumstances-based use of, 53
   computer-mediated, 95–96,
     108–109
   connotative, 47
   controlled-access, 6
   denotative, 47
   dialogic. *See* Dialogic
     communication
   feedback involved in, 44
   integrated marketing, 96
   mediated, 9
   self-replicating, 97
   symmetrical models of, 44
   transparency in, 65
   two-way, 49

153

Communication management, 32
Community
  building of, 117
  online, 127–128
Computer-mediated
    communication, 95–96, 108–109
Computer server, 30
Conductor typology, 33–34, 36
Connotative meaning, 47, 49
Consumer-generated media, 94–95
Content analysis, 147
Content management systems,
    6–7, 126
Contingency interactivity, 10–11
Contingency public relations, 11
Controlled-access communication, 6
Control mutuality, 67, 69, 115
Convergence, 39
Conversations, markets as, 52–53
Corporate bloggers, 7
Creator typology, 47–48
Crises, 128–129
Culture
  in media relations, 83–85
  as relational antecedent, 63–66
Cybernetics, 18–19
Cyber public relations, 10
Cyberwarfare, 116

Databases, 34
Deadlines, 83
Denotative meaning, 47, 49
Dialogic communication
  definition of, 49
  generating return visits through,
    51–52
  rhetorical importance of, 131
  useful information, 50
Dialogic loop, 50
Disaster planning, 129
Distributed public relations, 98
Diversity, 83–85
Document-based lessons, 126
Domain names, 17
Dot-orgs, 99

EDGAR, 100
E-mail
  definition of, 5
  news releases using, 39
  online memo use of, 37
Emergencies, 128–129
Employee relations, 11
Equivocality, 61
Evaluation
  description of, 23
  research methods for.
    See Research methods
  timing of, 148
  value in, 138–139
Exchange relationships, 69
Executive showcasing, 84
Experiments, 141–142
Externals, 22
Extranets, 6, 94
E-zines, 38–39

Facilitator typology, 48–49
Feedback, 44
Feeds, 7–8, 80
File transfer protocol. *See* FTP
Fluff, 36
Focus groups, 142–145
Forums, 6, 92–93
Frequently asked questions,
  91–92
FTP, 5, 38
Functional interactivity, 10

GDTs. *See* Geographically
  dispersed teams
General-access facts, 91–92
Geographical diversity, 83–84
Geographically dispersed
  teams, 127
Glocalization, 97–98
Goals
  objectives vs., 125
  systems focus on, 18
Grassroots media, 65
Group blogs, 63–64

HTML. *See* Hypertext markup
    language
Hyperlinking, 17
Hypertext markup language,
    38, 100
Hypertext transfer protocol, 5

Information
    access to, 81
    accuracy of, 83
    dissemination of, 37–39
    equivocality of, 61
    gathering of, 34–35
    newsworthy content, 81–82
    organizational, 112–113
    packaging of, 36–37
    sources of, 79–80, 85
    usefulness of, 50–51
Informational boundary
    spanning, 21
Information production
    fields, 44
Instant messaging, 5–6
Integrated marketing
    communication, 96
Interactive media, 108–109
Interactivity
    contingency, 10–11
    description of, 9, 148
    functional, 10
Internal publics, 96–97
Internals, 21–22
International public relations, 107
Internet
    access to, 107
    database functions of, 34
    definition of, 5, 47
    evolution of, 8
    growth of, 35–36
    hopes and expectations for, 4
    lack of systematic editorial
        controls, 108
    negotiation uses of, 108
    peace-making uses of, 117
    search engines, 17

Internet forums, 6
Internet relay chats. *See* Chats
Interpersonal communication, 4
Interviewer bias, 144
Interviews, 142–145
Intranets
    communicative uses of, 16, 93–94
    definition of, 6
    privacy benefits of, 93–94
Investors, 99
Issue-driven relationships
    in adversarial organizations,
        114–117
    in alliances, 113
    interactive media, 108–109
    issues, 106
    online public relations in, 117
    overview of, 105
    peace making, 117
    technology and content required
        for, 107–108

Journalists, 82–83

Koch, Howard, 2–3

"Magic bullet" theory, 3
Managers, 21–22
Marketing, 51–52
Marketplace changes, 19–20
Markets as conversations, 52–53
Mass communication, 4
Media relations
    culture in, 83–85
    online, 38
Media richness theory, 61–62
Mediated communication, 9

National diversity, 83–84
News alerts, 80
News cycle, 79–80
News-driven relationships
    alerts, 80
    antecedents of, 76–85
    feeds, 80

156   PUBLIC RELATIONS ONLINE

journalists, 82–83
newsworthy content, 81–82
press releases, 78
publicity, 75–76
really simple syndication, 80–81
Web sites, 76
Newsletters, 38
News media Web sites, 76
News releases
  e-mail, 39
  online, 38, 78
  video, 38
Newsworthy content, 81–82
Nonprofit organizations, 99, 113
Nonverbal cues, during
    interviews, 144

Objectives, 125
Online clipping and tracking
    services, 146
Online community, 127–128
Online forums, 92–93
Online media. *See also* Internet
  access to, 61, 107
  choices for using, 54
  circumstances-based use of, 53
  defining of, 4–8
  "de-massification" of, 9
  employee relations affected
      by, 11
  interactivity of. *See* Interactivity
  lack of systematic editorial
      controls, 108
  media richness theory, 61–62
Online media relations, 38
Online news releases, 38
Online organizations, 106
Online pressrooms, 77
Online public relations. *See also*
    Public relations
  in issue-driven relationships, 117
  one-way approaches to, 30–32
  systems theory importance to,
      24–25
  vignette about, 1–2

Online publics, 106
Online relationships.
    See Relationship(s)
Online teamwork, 126–127
Openness, 67–68, 131
Open-source software,
    64–65, 132
Open systems, 18, 23
Opt-in news service, 80
Organization(s)
  activist, 113
  adversarial, 114–117
  conflict in, 116–117
  culture of, 63–66, 97
  diversity of, 84–85
  individual's identification
      with, 63
  information conducted and
      gathered by, 112–113
  nonprofit, 99, 113
  online, 106
  public and, 47, 70, 106, 112
  real-time responses by,
      124–125
  relationships. *See* Relationship(s)

Peace making, 117
Peer-to-peer public relations,
    44, 86
Personal influence model, 83
Ping, 8
Planning
  for crises, 128–129
  description of, 23
  for disasters, 129
  for emergencies, 128–129
  evaluative questions used in,
      126–127
  goals and objectives developed
      through, 125
  Web site creation, 125–127
Podcasts, 8
Positivity, 67–68, 130–131
Press agentry, 30–31
Press releases, 78–79

Proactive strategies, 23
Proprietary software, 65–66
PR Relationship Measurement Scale,
  67, 69
PSAs. *See* Public service
  announcements
Pseudo-experiments, 141
Public(s)
  active, 112–113
  internal, 96–97
  issues for, 106
  online, 106
  organization and, 47, 70,
    106, 112
  situational theory of, 109
Public information, 31–32
Publicity, 30–31, 75–76, 86, 125
Public relations. *See also* Online
  public relations
  communal relationships
    promoted by, 70
  contingency, 11
  cybernetics in, 19
  definition of, 9
  focus of, 25
  four-step process involved
    in, 23
  generating return visits goal of,
    51–52
  Grunig and Hunt model of, 45
  marketing vs., 51
  personal influence model
    of, 83
  publicity function of, 30–31
  strategic, 86
  two-way asymmetrical, 45–46
  two-way symmetrical, 46–47
Public relations people
  boundary spanning by, 20–21
  journalists vs., 82
  managers, 21–22
  technicians, 21–22
  typologies of. *See* Typologies
Public service announcements,
  38–39

Pull media, 23–24, 82
Push media, 24, 82

Reactive strategies, 23
Really simple syndication, 7–8, 80–81
Real-time discussion, 143
Relational antecedents
  cultures, 63–66
  individuals, 63
  open-source and, 64
  overview of, 60
  technologies, 60–63
Relational databases, 35
Relational maintenance strategies,
  66–68
Relationship(s)
  in alliances, 113
  among adversarial organizations,
    114–117
  benefits of, 67
  commerce-driven.
    See Commerce-driven
    relationships
  commitment in, 69
  communal, 69–70
  control mutuality in, 67, 69
  definition of, 59–60
  evaluation of, 67, 69–70
  exchange, 69
  focus on, 59–60
  issue-drive. *See* Issue-driven
    relationships
  maintaining of, 66–68
  news-driven. *See* News-driven
    relationships
  organization-public, 67, 70
  satisfaction in, 69
  source-reporter, 76
  studying of, 60
  trust in, 69
Relationship building
  communication technologies
    for, 61
  description of, 9
  processes involved in, 66–67

Representational boundary
spanning, 21
Research, 23, 138
Researcher-defined research
spaces, 143
Research methods
content analysis, 147
description of, 138
experiments, 141–142
focus groups, 142–145
interviews, 142–145
online clipping and tracking
services, 146
server data, 146
surveys, 139–141
unobtrusive types of, 145–147
usability testing, 138, 145
Response rates, of surveys,
140–141
RSS. *See* Really simple
syndication

Sampling
for surveys, 139–141
for usability testing, 145
Satisfaction, 69
Search engines, 17
Self-replicating communication, 97
Server-client relationship, 30
Server data, 146
Server-side public relations, 30, 76
Sharing tasks, 67–68, 132
Situational theory of publics, 109
Social networks
analysis of, 147
description of, 67–68, 109–111,
132–133
Source-reporter relationships, 76
Steward typology, 32–33
Streaming audio and video,
39–40
Structuration, 65
Subject-defined research
spaces, 143
Subsystems, 17

Super users, 138–139
Suprasystems, 17
Surveys, 139–141
Symmetrical public relations,
46–47
Systems
boundaries, 17
closed, 18, 23
collaboration in, 132–133
concepts associated with, 16–18
definition of, 16
description of, 15–16, 132
example of, 18–20
goal-directed nature of, 18
hierarchy of, 17
homeostasis of, 17–18
online public relations and,
24–25
open, 18, 23
purposeful activity of, 18
self-regulation of, 23

Task sharing, 67–68, 132
Teamwork, online, 126–127
Technicians, 21–22
Thread, 6
Throughput, 17
Town crier typology, 32
Trackback, 8
Traffic manager typology, 33
Transparency, 65
Trust, 69
Two-way asymmetrical public
relations, 45–46
Two-way communication, 49
Two-way symmetrical public
relations, 46–47
Two-way typologies, 47–53
Typologies
conductor, 33–34, 36
creator, 47–48
definition of, 32
facilitator, 48–49
steward, 32–33
town crier, 32

traffic manager, 33
two-way, 47–53

URLs, 5
Usability testing, 138, 145
Usefulness of information, 50–51

Video, streaming, 39–40
Video-based real-time conferencing, 143
Video news releases, 38

Web 2.0, 148
Web logs. *See* Blogs
Webmaster, 33

Web pages, commerce-driven, 90–91
Web sites
building of, 125–127
common features of, 113–115
information obtained from, 15–16
news media, 76
Welles, Orson, 2–3
Wiki, 7, 132
Wikipedia, 7
Wire services, 78
World Wide Web, 5

XBRL, 100

Y2K crisis, 3

About the Author

Tom Kelleher rejoined the School of Communications at the University of Hawai'i at Manoa in fall 2006 after two years on the faculty at the University of North Carolina at Chapel Hill. He started at Hawai'i in 1999 after earning his PhD from the University of Florida. He has taught courses in introductory public relations, public relations writing, advanced public relations, online communication, communication campaigns, media effects, honors research, and communication theory.

Kelleher has published in *Journal of Public Relations Research, Public Relations Review, Journal of Computer-Mediated Communication, Journal of Mass Media Ethics, Journal of Communication Management*, and *Teaching Public Relations.* He has worked in university relations at the University of Florida; science communication at NASA in Huntsville, Alabama; and agency public relations at Ketchum in Atlanta. He also has consulted for various university-related organizations in Honolulu, Hawai'i. His research interests are online public relations, public relations theory, campaigns, ethics, and teaching and learning with online media.

He likes surfing in the ocean more than surfing online, but still manages to do some of both.